CW00801493

)

MAGNIFY THE LORD

Luke 1:46-55

DR MARTYN LLOYD-JONES

BRYNTIRION PRESS

CHRISTIAN
HERITAGE

Copyright © Martyn Lloyd-Jones 2011

ISBN 978-1-84550-754-1

10 9 8 7 6 5 4 3 2 1

First published in 1998
© Elizabeth Catherwood and Ann Lockwood

Reprinted in 2011
by
Christian Focus Publications,
Geanies House, Fearn,
Ross-shire, IV20 1TW, Scotland
www.christianfocus.com
with
Bryntirion Press
Pen-y-bont ar Ogwr/Bridgend
CF31 4DX, Wales, Great Britain

Cover design
by
Daniel van Straaten

Printed by
Bell and Bain, Glasgow

CONTENTS

FOREWORD

When I imagine the author of the book you're holding right now, the first thing I think of is a 'gentle steamroller'. It was very early in my ministry – I was a seminary student in New Orleans – and I came across a book about the famous Welsh preacher D. Martyn Lloyd-Jones. In those days, I was seeking to find my way as a preacher, trying to pray and discern how I could have the kind of ministry that would last in its work for the kingdom of Christ. I read a lot of biographies of pastors and teachers from the past, men I admired and wanted, in some way, to be like. With Lloyd-Jones, one phrase struck me: a gentle steamroller.

Lloyd-Jones hosted a Friday night discussion at his church, Westminster Chapel in London. These events were quite different, it seems, from his Sunday morning expositions, such as you find in this book. Here there was the opportunity for dialogue, conversation, questions, and even debate over issues of the Bible, theology, and the living of life. One man who had sat through these discussions for a long time, noted that he had never raised his voice to ask a question or to participate in the discussion. When Mrs Lloyd-Jones asked him the reason for his silence, this man remembered, he replied that he 'considered it unwise to stand in the path of a steamroller'. This man quickly clarified with words that have embedded themselves in my memory for now nearly eighteen years. 'But the Doctor was a very gentle steamroller, and he was particularly kind to the young and weak in the faith.'[1]

When I say I think of a 'gentle steamroller,' I mean that I think of that phrase, not the actual thing since, of course, I can't comprehend how something could be simultaneously 'gentle' and a 'steamroller.' That, though, was the point. No one can. What makes something 'gentle' means it cannot really be a 'steamroller' and vice-versa. But, in the life of this preacher, one man sensed a combination of dynamism and gentleness that

---

1   Christopher Catherwood, *Martyn Lloyd-Jones: A Family Portrait* (Grand Rapids: Baker, 1994), p. 180.

he put into words with that paradox. I have hoped, but I'm sure never attained, in my ministry the blessing by the Holy Spirit to be a gentle steamroller of the gospel of Christ Jesus.

That paradox though wasn't unique to Lloyd-Jones. What this man saw from the pews in London was the Spirit wrestling a preacher into the image of his Christ (Rom. 8:29). Jesus, after all, is described in similar terms of a seeming contradiction. He is both predator and prey, priest and offering, king and slave. He is seen in the pages of Scripture evoking the kind of terror from which people flee to the mountains for escape (Luke 21:20-22), and the kind of tenderness with which he washes the dung and dust from his students' feet (John 13:1-17). But the complexity of Jesus can be disorienting, and Lloyd-Jones never shrank from this disorientation, either in exposition or emulation.

I felt something of this tension several years ago as I found myself preaching through a series on the Book of Revelation. This series was long by my standards, though nowhere nearly as long as the years and years in Bible passages preached through by Lloyd-Jones. I'm sure he would have dismissed my series as a 'brief overview'. Nonetheless, I wrestled with whether to take a break in this preaching because Christmastime was drawing near. Holiday cheer was all around, from the sounds of Bing Crosby crooning 'O Little Town of Bethlehem' on the music loop at the grocery store to the inflatable Santa in front of the house two doors down from mine. Here I was preaching on Jesus as conquering Warrior-Messiah, dripped in blood and destroying his enemies. It seemed a little out of kilter for the time of year.

Shouldn't I take a break, I wondered, from the Apocalypse to highlight the little Lord Jesus asleep on the hay? Wasn't there something kind of, well, unseasonable about teaching, at this time of year, about a Christ who bears a sword and a cosmic entourage, who prepares his people a messianic banquet and then prepares the birds a banquet of the flesh and blood of his enemies (Rev. 19:17-19)? It's hard, after all, to imagine Tiny Tim exclaiming 'God bless us every one' after hearing my lessons on southern-fried Gog and Magog.

Jesus, though, refuses to fit into our Procrustean beds. The gentleness of Jesus, abstracted from everything else, oozes into an unbiblical and tepid sentimentalism. And the power of Jesus, isolated from the rest of him, gives a twisted, hyper-masculinized, and foreboding picture of our Christ as pugilist and even thug.

The antidote to these polarities is found in the song of a young virgin of Nazareth, a woman whose life has just been upended by a mysterious messenger from beyond the skies, and by a long-promised Embryo growing within her midsection. The book you hold will guide you through that song, and will teach you to sing it with her. Here the Blessed Virgin Mary combines joy at a promise-keeping God with the awe that his kingdom means the uprooting of every rival throne. Here there is gentleness – the kind of quiet beauty of the heart the Scripture commends in the godly woman (1 Pet. 3:1-4) – and there is also a call to arms – the kind of 'spiritual warfare' the Scripture calls us to join (Eph. 6:10-20).

For too many evangelicals, what we call 'the Magnificat' is a mystery. Some are so paranoid about distinguishing themselves from the Marian devotion of other churches that they see Mary as a minor supporting actress in the drama of redemption. She's the Catholic relative they're glad to see at the Christmas party, but they don't want to ask to pray. But it isn't the Bishop of Rome but the angel of God who tells us that every generation should call Mary 'blessed' (Luke 1:48b), or that she is greatly honored above all women (Luke 1:28, 30). If we will listen to her, and sing with her, we can grow to see the offspring of the woman in all his might and all his fragility, in his justice and in his mercy. This book will drive you to that Virgin's Song – and beyond it, to the gospel, in ways you don't expect by walking you through the tension between Bethlehem and Armageddon.

In the end, I decided not to take a break from Revelation for Christmas. And it was the Magnificat that changed my mind, for many of the reasons the great Lloyd-Jones lays out with such clarity in this book. The Mother of our Lord set the tone when she sang of God's mercy to his people, of his faithfulness to his covenant promises. And then she sang also of the truth that in this fetal Incarnate One within her God 'has shown strength with his arm; he has scattered the proud in the thoughts of their hearts; he has brought down the mighty from their thrones, and exalted those of humble estate; he has filled the hungry with good things, and the rich he has sent away' (Luke 1:51-53). Come to think of it, she sounds like a rather gentle steamroller. No wonder the Doctor understood her so well.

Russell D. Moore
DEAN, THE SOUTHERN BAPTIST THEOLOGICAL SEMINARY, LOUISVILLE, KENTUCKY

1

MAGNIFYING GOD

'And Mary said, My soul doth magnify the Lord, And my spirit hath rejoiced in God my Saviour. For he hath regarded the low estate of his handmaiden: for, behold, from henceforth all generations shall call me blessed. For he that is mighty hath done to me great things; and holy *is* his name. And his mercy *is* on them that fear him from generation to generation. He hath shewed strength with his arm; he hath scattered the proud in the imagination of their hearts. He hath put down the mighty from *their* seats, and exalted them of low degree. He hath filled the hungry with good things;

and the rich he hath sent empty away. He hath holpen his servant Israel, in remembrance of his mercy; As he spake to our fathers, to Abraham, and to his seed for ever' (Luke 1:46-55).

This statement, this bursting forth of Mary into worship and praise and adoration, which we call 'The Magnificat', is something which is worthy of our most careful consideration. There is, perhaps, no better way of approaching the season of Christmas than to do so in terms of a consideration of this particular passage. Indeed, I think we can say that there is no better test of our understanding of the meaning of the Incarnation, everything we think of and celebrate during these days, than our reaction to this song of Mary; because, as I want to try to show you, here, in this short compass, in a very extraordinary manner, she brings us face to face with some of the many central matters in connection with our salvation.

STAGES

There are many things which are of great interest with which we cannot stay; I merely note them in passing. It is very interesting, for instance, to notice the stages through which Mary herself passed in connection with this momentous event which was to take place. When, *first of all*, the archangel Gabriel went to her and made his announcement, Mary was incredulous; she was sceptical, she stumbled. The thing, of course, was so staggering, so unusual, so amazing that she could not receive it, and she made her protestation. Indeed, she virtually suggested to the angel that what he was saying was quite impossible. But the angel reminded her that 'with God nothing shall be impossible', that she must not think in those terms and in those categories. She must realise that here she was in a different realm: that he was no ordinary human emissary, nor the bearer of a message from any earthly or human power, but that he was the messenger of God.

Then, as a result of that, Mary moved on to this **second** stage in which she said: 'Behold the handmaid of the Lord, be it unto me according to thy word.' This is a most interesting process, so typical and characteristic of the way in which the gospel tends to come to all of us. At first it seems impossible. But then we feel rebuked for that and we say: 'Well, I don't understand it, but I will submit.' That is what Mary did. She still did not understand. 'All right', she seems to say: 'I hear what you have said to me, and I know that what you say is right concerning God, and that with God nothing is impossible. I therefore leave myself in God's hands, still not understanding, but ready to wait and to listen and to follow.' A most important step.

But then she went and visited her cousin Elisabeth, and, as the result of what happened to Elisabeth, and especially as the result of what Elisabeth said to her, Mary burst forth into this great song, this great hymn of praise. Elisabeth had turned to Mary and said: 'Blessed *art* thou among women, and blessed *is* the fruit of thy womb. And whence *is* this to me, that the mother of my Lord should come to me? For, lo, as soon as the voice of thy salutation sounded in mine ears, the babe leaped in my womb for joy. And blessed *is* she that believed: for there shall be a performance of those things which were told her from the Lord' (Luke 1:42-45).

And then we see that God used those very words of Elisabeth to confirm to Mary the announcement that had already been made by the archangel. They brought her to her real understanding, because the moment Elisabeth said that to her, we are told that Mary said: 'My soul doth magnify the Lord, And my spirit hath rejoiced in God my Saviour.' And she poured forth her heart in this extraordinary praise and adoration of God, and it is to this that I want to call your attention.

CHARACTERISTICS
So let us look at some of the characteristics of these words uttered by Mary.

Depth
First, let us notice the *depth of feeling* with which she spoke, which is conveyed in these words. She said: 'My soul doth magnify the Lord, And my spirit hath rejoiced in God my Saviour.' Now she drew a distinction between her soul and her spirit. This is a very interesting theological point. Again, we must not stay with this and we must not build too much upon it, but, at any rate, I think we are reminded here and elsewhere in Scripture that

14

whether the soul and spirit are essentially one or not, there is a distinction between them. The soul in general refers to the rational powers. When the expression soul is used in this way in contra-distinction to spirit, it is meant to refer to the intellect, to the feelings, to the way in which we correspond with one another and have fellowship and relationship with one another. The soul is essentially the rational part of man.

Then the spirit represents the perception. There is a difference between ability and understanding. There is a difference between knowledge and perception. The spirit is a higher faculty, a higher aspect of this possession which we all have. It includes the capacity for worship. The soul, in other words, is that which links us to all that is round and about us: to man and to animals; to history and to the world and all we can see. That is the soul. But if you want to argue that there are only two parts in man and not three, you must say, nevertheless, that there is this compartment, as it were, of the soul which enables one to appreciate the unseen and the spiritual, the spirit: everything that is greatest and uppermost in man.

So, Mary uses the two expressions, 'My soul' and 'my spirit', by which she means that she is moved in the very depth and centre of her being. She is not merely pleased in a general sense and on the surface. It is not merely something of general interest to her. She has a realisation of something that, she says, has touched her in the very centre and the most vital part of her personality. That is why all this is so important: that is the effect of the good news of salvation upon the soul. This is the effect to which it has always led when people have really understood what it is all about.

In other words, it is like the passage in Ephesians 5:19; there is all the difference between mere 'singing' and 'making melody' in our hearts. The heart includes this same thing: the soul and spirit, the very centre of man's whole personality. And it is here that this response to the gospel really comes forth. That is where it has its origin. So we find Mary obviously stirred to the very depths of her soul, and the result is that she speaks with a sense of dignity and of greatness, as she is aware of something profound. You cannot read through what she said without sensing her feeling of awe and of wonder, of worship and of amazement. 'This', she seems to be saying, 'is the most amazing thing I have ever known. I am beyond and beside myself. My soul and my spirit.'

There, then, is the first thing that emerges and the first thing, therefore, by which we test ourselves. You have but to read the New Testament to see that all the men and women who truly have understood the gospel have said something similar; even the Psalmist, looking forward to it, says: 'Bless the LORD, O my soul: and all that is within me, *bless* his holy name' (Ps. 103:1).

I could quote hymns to you; I could quote statements to you from the saints throughout the centuries. They are all saying the same thing and, of course, it must be true. If we really understand what happened when the Son of God left the courts of heaven and came into the world in this way and manner, if we grasp something of its eternal significance, of its profundity, its amazing character, how can it fail to move us, especially in our souls and in our spirits?

And here we are again reminded of how this Christmas season can be so abused even in the church, with men and women talking about themselves and about one another. No, no! It is not just a feeling of goodwill and of friendliness and of happiness; it is something, if we really get hold of it, that moves us in the soul and in the spirit.

Manifestation

Then, *secondly*, look for a moment at *the manifestation of this feeling*. Two words stand out. The first is the element of adoration: 'My soul doth magnify the Lord'. Now this is an extraordinary expression. It means to make great and to make glorious. 'But,' says someone, 'what a foolish term. How can one magnify God? How can a human being, a creature, one who is but a Creator-created being, how can such a one magnify, make great, multiply, as it were, the Lord God Almighty?' Of course, in an ultimate sense, it cannot be done, and Mary realises that, as all the psalmists who used the term realised it. And yet there is a sense in which it is very true because while we cannot do anything as such to God in his greatness and in his majesty, we can help other people to see it. We can, as it were, act as a kind of lens that makes him greater in the eyes and in the esteem and in the sight of people.

And that is what Mary was trying to express. It is as if she were saying: 'How can I make known what I have seen of the greatness and of the glory of God? I want everybody to know this: I want everybody to see it. "My soul doth magnify the Lord". I am clutching at every word that I can get hold of in order to express something of his greatness and his glory.'

It is, then, a very profound way of giving expression to this depth of desire that God might be known and might be seen, that what he is might be shown in a large way and painted on an enormous canvas, that the whole world may see it and look at it and bow before him in adoration and in praise. 'My soul doth magnify the Lord...'

So what about us? I am simply taking these words and holding them before you in order that we may examine ourselves in the light of them. Do our souls magnify the Lord? Is this our innermost desire? The Psalmist has expressed it: 'O magnify the LORD with me' (Ps. 34:3). 'Let us do it together,' he says, 'let everybody join in. Let us make his name great. Let us hold it before the nations and the peoples.'

The other word is *rejoice*. 'My soul doth magnify the Lord, And my spirit hath rejoiced in God my

Saviour.' Now the word 'rejoice' is not quite good enough; it is not quite strong enough. The word really means to exult in him or to make your boasting of him. This is the thing in which I exult. The world is always exulting in various things and men make their proud boast of themselves. But: 'O,' says Mary, 'my spirit exults in God. Here is the theme of my rejoicing – in God my Saviour.'

Significance

Cause

Thirdly, let us go on to see the full significance of this. What is the cause of this feeling within her? And here we come to what I want to emphasise particularly. Why is Mary magnifying the Lord? Why does her spirit exult in God her Saviour? And she really supplies us with the answer. It is not primarily because of what has happened to her. She does mention that: it comes in, but that is merely an incident in her hymn of praise. So what is the cause of her adoration, of her praise? It is because God himself is who and what he is, and because of what he is doing with respect to the world. Mary's eye, in other words, is not upon herself. You see how certain parts of the Church have so abused and made an utter travesty of this. Mary is full of humility. She refers to herself as what she is – 'the low estate of thine handmaiden'. There is nothing here about the 'mother of God' and about 'the queen of heaven'. Mary is not thinking about herself. Mary has seen something that makes her forget herself; and this is the ultimate test of a true understanding of what happened when God in the fulness of the times 'sent forth his Son, made of a woman, made under the law' (Gal. 4:4). Mary is rejoicing not so much in the fact that she is to be given this great privilege, she has been reminded by Elisabeth of what that is and of how people are going to call her blessed, and she repeats that: 'from henceforth all generations shall call me blessed'. But that is not the thing that really moves her. It is what God is doing: this historic event, this climactic action of God himself. She is humbled and grateful at the thought of the fact that she is to be given a part and a place in this, but it is the thing itself that moves her and makes her sing and worship. She is filled with a sense of amazement, of worship, adoration and utter astonishment. She sees the inner meaning of the action. She has a glimpse and a glimmering of understanding of the whole purpose of salvation, what God is doing in bringing forth his Son into the world, even out of her womb.

Now that is the secret of this song. And it is also the secret of the whole Christian position. What is it that leads to worship and to praise, to exultation, to adoration? And the answer is that it is always the understanding. The only singing that is of any value in the sight of God is that which is based upon the understanding, the understanding of the truth. That is why we must take this occasion to remind ourselves, therefore, that we must never go for the emotions directly. We must never go for the will directly. The emotions and the will are the result of something seen by the understanding.

That is what Elisabeth shows. She was filled with the Holy Spirit, we are told, and she spoke forth with understanding – enlightenment of the Spirit. And exactly the same thing is true here of Mary. And what Mary sees is not that she is to be made great because she has this privilege, but the greatness of the God who is acting and the greatness of the action which he is taking.

Expression

So, **fourthly**, let us follow her in *the expression of her feeling*. What does she say? The main thing here, of course, is that Mary is telling us certain things about God as he is. She is adoring God for being what he is, and this is the very essence of Christian worship and of Christian praise. Alas, in our weakness and frailty, we are so concerned about the benefits that we forget the giver. But here is adoration and worship at its very best. There are two dangers which confront us: there is the danger to which I have already referred – the monstrosity of the false teaching and the exaggeration of the Roman Catholic Church. But let us be careful also that in a violent reaction against that we do not underestimate what Mary saw and what she expressed in the Magnificat. Let us keep to the balance of the Scriptures and not be governed by prejudices.

And here, Mary is expressing the very heart and soul of Christian praise and worship and adoration. God himself. *First and foremost*, his greatness and his glory: 'My soul doth *magnify* the Lord' (emphasis added). There is nothing above that; we will never rise above that; to magnify the *Lord*. The Lord is Jehovah, and he is to be magnified and praised and worshipped because of that. Who is he? He says: 'I AM THAT I AM' (Exod. 3:14). There is the element in it, also, of 'I am what I shall become'. But the great central thing is that he is from eternity to eternity. 'I am that I am' – the Lord. 'Great *is* the LORD,' says the Psalmist, 'and greatly to be praised' (Ps. 48:1).

So we have not understood the meaning of Christmas unless we come there. We do not stop in the stable and with the manger. Of course we must go there, but what we see there is this great God, the Lord. And the moment you do that, you get your right perspective, you get your right way of looking at things. Have we not reached a terrible pass when it is essential to remind Christian people that they must not allow their thinking to be governed by the world at a time like this, but by the Scripture and its teaching. And this is the scriptural way: you start with this Lord, you magnify him. He is responsible for everything that has happened. It is his action. He is the one who is ultimately to be praised.

Then, take the **second** term she uses, *Saviour*. 'My soul', she says, 'doth magnify the Lord, And

my spirit hath rejoiced in God my Saviour.' What
does the term *Saviour* mean? It is a great term
used everywhere in the Bible concerning God. It
means the one who delivers, the one who keeps.
We have a wonderful summary of Old Testament
history in this Magnificat. What Mary is saying,
in effect, is this: 'O God, my soul magnifies you,
because I can see now that you are doing what you
have always done. You are always the same. You
have been doing it throughout the centuries, but
now here is the climax, and it is the climax of all
that has gone before.'

The Saviour. That was God's character with
respect to Israel, was it not? Read the Old Testament! It is a history of God ever delivering these
people. Look how he delivered them out of the
captivity and the bondage of Egypt. They would
have perished there, it would have been the end.
So how did they come out? How did they ever go
to the land Canaan, the land of possession? It was
God the Saviour who brought them out with his
strong arm. The Saviour! Of course!

And so he continued to be. How often did he
deliver them from their cruel enemies? How often
did he vanquish mighty enemy armies when
they were comparatively defenceless? Read the
historical books and you will see God the Saviour.
Mary sees all this. And then go on and see how,
even from the captivity of Babylon, he brought
back a remnant to carry on his purpose. It is
always God the Saviour. And thus the Psalmist

23

says very rightly: 'he that keepeth Israel shall neither slumber nor sleep' (Ps. 121:4). Even when they were rebellious and sinful he kept his eye upon them. He allowed things to go so far but never further. He allowed enemies to arise and conquer them, but never to destroy them. He is the Saviour of his people; he is the shepherd of the flock: 'my Saviour'. Mary sees it. And now she suddenly sees that God is doing this on an infinitely bigger scale. 'What is this action? What is he doing to me?' she seems to say. Ah! this is a part of his salvation for the world. God my Saviour.

Thirdly, she pays special attention to his *power*. She is very impressed by this. Listen to her: 'he that is mighty hath done to me great things' (v. 49). And again in verse 51: 'He hath shewed strength with his arm; he hath scattered the proud in the imagination of their hearts.' He that is mighty! It is not surprising that she emphasises this; it is this, if I may so put it, that enables God to be the Saviour. If this were not true of God he could not be the Saviour, and this is what is especially needed by the world; it is the thing that is so especially needed by all of us.

Why does she magnify the Lord for his greatness, for his power and for his strength? Well, she contrasts it with her own weakness and with the utter weakness and helplessness and hopelessness of the world. The hope for the world is the power of God, the strength of his arm. He that is mighty. He is almighty. The angel had reminded

24

her of that. She had stumbled; she had said: 'How can this be seeing that I know not a man? You are telling me that I am to bring forth a son but I am a virgin, I have never known a man. How can this be? The thing is impossible.' And the answer is that 'With God nothing shall be impossible.' Thank God!

Here is the assurance of salvation. It is the might and strength of God. 'I am not ashamed of the gospel of Christ', says Paul. Why? '[F]or it is the power of God unto salvation to every one that believeth' (Rom. 1:16). The power! And Mary's soul magnifies the Lord because of this – and so should ours!

Look at it like this: the world is as it is because it is in the grip and under the power of the devil and of hell. The devil is 'the god of this world' (2 Cor. 4:4). He is 'the prince of the power of the air, the spirit that now worketh in the children of disobedience' (Eph. 2:2), and his power is a mighty power. Read your Old Testament. Look at him as he tempts the greatest patriarchs and saints. They fell before him in utter weakness and helpless-less. '[W]e wrestle not against flesh and blood, but against principalities, against the powers, against the rulers of the darkness of this world, against spiritual wickedness in high *places*' (Eph. 6:12).

Is there any hope for the world? Does it lie in international conferences? Does it lie in the future? No it does not! The world goes round and round in circles; it lacks the power to deal with the situation.

But, thank God, we are reminded of one that is mighty. 'He hath shewed strength with his arm; he hath scattered the proud in the imagination of their hearts.' He is the almighty one.

That is the first and primary name that is used with respect to God in the Bible. It is the word *El*, and it means the strong one. When God was revealing himself to the people that is the name he used: I am the strong one; the almighty.

And so the archangel Gabriel is reminding Mary of something that is crucial and vital in this whole situation. There would be no salvation for this world were it not that God is the mighty one, the almighty, and what he is doing there in Bethlehem is manifesting his power, 'the power of God unto salvation' (Rom. 1:16). It is an extraordinary thing and a still more extraordinary way of doing it, but that is what he is doing. God is putting into motion his plan and it is working out according to his power.

Then, *fourthly*, she speaks of his *holiness*. '[H]e that is mighty hath done to me great things' – and then – 'and holy *is* his name'. I wonder whether you have ever stopped at that and asked the question, Why does she say that? Why does she bring that in at all? And you notice especially that she connects it with the power by means of the word *and*. 'I magnify the Lord', she says, 'not only for his power but also for his holiness.' This, again, is one of the keys to the understanding of the whole purpose of salvation. Why is there salvation? Why did God ever send his only Son into this world? Why was there ever a cross on Calvary's hill?

And, in the last analysis, this is the answer: because God is holy. Because his name is holy. The Bible puts this in many ways: 'God is light,' it says, 'and in him is no darkness at all' (1 John 1:5). He is 'a consuming fire' (Heb. 12:29). That is an expression of God's holiness. 'But what has it got to do with salvation?' asks someone. It is this: God is eternally opposed to sin. He hates it. And it is because he hates it that there is salvation. God made the world; made it perfect; there was nothing wrong; there was no blemish; he looked at it and saw that it was good. Ah! but sin came in. The devil introduced evil; sin has become rampant; evil is widespread and God in his holiness cannot tolerate it. It is because God hates sin with all the intensity of his holy nature that there is salvation.

Indeed, I do not hesitate to make a statement like this: it is because his name is holy that he *must* deal with sin, that he *must* bring in redemption. God, being God, cannot leave the world as it is, in sin, under the power of the devil, ruled by the god of this world. No, no, that is utterly opposed to him and he hates it and he will get rid of it. His name is holy, and because it is, he has done what he has done; and everything God does is holy. It is not merely powerful, it is holy.

Notice how the archangel Gabriel put it to Mary herself? He said: 'The Holy Ghost shall come upon thee'. And then that amazing expression, 'that holy thing which shall be born of thee'. Everything about this salvation is holy. Jesus Christ was perfect. There was no sin in him. He did not inherit the sin that was in Adam's nature. He was pure, he was holy, and right through the whole of his teaching and in every thing that he did, this element of holiness always comes out. There he was, born as a babe: yes, but he was not an ordinary babe. He was separate from sin, separate from sinners, no sin in him – holy.

Then move on to the cross: what is happening there? Ah, it is the same element of holiness that I see. It is God's hatred of sin; God punishing sin; God getting rid of sin. '[H]oly *is* his name.' Everything in connection with this great movement of salvation from beginning to end is characterised by holiness.

But, *fifthly*, there is yet another term. Listen to it! It is the wonderful term *mercy*. 'And his mercy *is* on them that fear him from generation to generation.' Once more I ask you to notice the word *and* at the beginning of that fiftieth verse: 'And his mercy *is* on them that fear him from generation to generation.' Thank God for this 'And'. If God were only almighty and holy, there would be no hope for us at all. If it were only true to say of God that he is the mighty one, that he is holy and of such a pure countenance that he cannot even look upon sin, we would not be considering this together now. We would not sing hymns of praise in the name of the Lord Jesus Christ. Why? Because if God were only almighty and holy, we should all be blotted out; the whole world would be destroyed and there would be no salvation. But thank God for this little 'And'. He is mighty, great in power, glorious in holiness and in majesty, *and* full of mercy and full of compassion. This is what saves us.

What does mercy mean? Perhaps the best way to answer that question is to consider it in the light of the word 'grace'. Grace and mercy go to-gether, and grace comes before mercy. Grace is love and favour towards those who do not deserve it because of their guilt. Grace is kindness and goodness revealed to those who do not deserve it because they are guilty. That is what grace means.

What is mercy? Well, mercy means love toward those who are not merely guilty but who are miserable in their guilt. That is the difference between grace and mercy. Grace is more general; mercy is particular. His mercy means that God looks down and sees mankind in its misery, in its agony, in its pain.

Now, of course, as I have already reminded you, Mary is summarising the whole history of the Old Testament. God said to Moses when he called him to deliver the children of Israel: 'I have surely seen the affliction of my people which are in Egypt, and have heard their cry by reason of their taskmasters; for I know their sorrows.' If that does not melt us and break us, what can? That is mercy.

This great, self-existent God who is from eternity to eternity, everlasting in his holiness and in his glory; the God who could exist apart from man and who does not need man. He created man and man in his folly fell into sin, and there he is in his misery and unhappiness and wretchedness, and this august, eternal God says: 'I have surely seen the affliction of my people ...'

That is why Jesus was born in Bethlehem. That is why he came so willingly. That is why he laid aside the signs of his glory and humbled himself and made himself of no reputation. God had seen our misery. Not only our guilt, but our misery also, our unhappiness, our wretchedness: the state of the world as the result of sin, as John Milton puts it in his hymn:

> He hath with a piteous eye,
> Looked upon our misery.
> For His mercies aye endure,
> Ever faithful, ever sure.

Mary praises God for his mercy, his compassion, for his piteous eye.

Finally, there is his *faithfulness*. 'He hath holpen his servant Israel, in remembrance of *his* mercy; As he spake to our fathers, to Abraham, and to his seed for ever.' God never forgets his promises. He had promised that he would visit and redeem his people, and Mary suddenly sees that what is happening to her is a part of this fulfilment of the promises of God.

All the Old Testament prophets had been waiting and longing and crying out, as it were, 'O come, O come, Immanuel'. When will he come? God has promised him. When will he appear? She realises that, at last, he is about to appear, that the holy thing that is to be born out of her womb is God's 'yea and amen' to all the promises that he had made, beginning in the Garden of Eden itself and continuing through prophets and seers and sages and kings and psalmists. Even unto this very hour God 'hath visited and redeemed his people'.

That is why Mary speaks as she does. That is why she says: 'My soul doth magnify the Lord, And my spirit hath rejoiced in God my Saviour.' The almighty. The holy one. The one who has mercy and compassion, who for his great love wherewith he loved us has sent his only Son not only into the world but even to the death of the cross. Great in might; great in mercy. O the riches of his grace, the unsearchable riches of his grace toward us in his Son, our Lord and Saviour Jesus Christ!

Have you seen it? Mary saw it in a flash. She had stumbled at first; she could not see it. But at last she sees it, the movement of God in salvation, and that is her response: 'My soul doth magnify the Lord, And my spirit hath rejoiced in God my Saviour.'

Has it come to you like that? Meditate upon it. Meditate upon it in terms of Scripture. See that it ever leads you to God who in his glory, in his majesty, has looked upon us and the world with such a piteous eye as to send his only Son into it for our redemption.

2

THE WISDOM OF GOD

'He hath shewed strength with his arm; he hath scattered the proud in the imagination of their hearts. He hath put down the mighty from *their* seats, and exalted them of low degree. He hath filled the hungry with good things; and the rich he hath sent empty away' (Luke 1:51-53)

We turn now to these particular words, this particular section, in Mary's great statement in the Magnificat, because I want to show you that it helps us to see and to realise what are, after all, some of the central principles in connection with this gospel of our Lord and Saviour Jesus Christ.

Now, the kind of person whom I find it very difficult to understand is the one who does not believe in the devil: 'the prince of the power of the air' (Eph. 2:2), the controller of the forces of evil and of sin. I find it difficult to understand such a person, simply because the devil's activity is so obvious and his working should surely be quite self-evident to everybody. But there is no point, perhaps, during the whole of the year; there is no aspect of the Christian gospel in which one sees so clearly the working, the efforts and the evil results of such efforts on the part of the devil, as in connection with this season of advent: this time of Christmas, when the Church throughout the world thinks in particular of the coming of the Son of God into this world, the birth of the Lord Jesus Christ in Bethlehem.

THE REAL MEANING OF CHRISTMAS

Is it not obvious to us that the real meaning of this great event – in many ways the central event in the whole history of the human race – is so largely obscured? People think of it in one of two main ways: some evaporate this great event into just some vague general feeling of goodwill, good cheer, happiness, an occasion for drink and a spirit of friendliness. That, I suppose, as regards the world in general, is the main notion and idea concerning the meaning of Christmas. It is just that and no more.

But then there are others, and this is a large group also, who seem to think that the central purpose of this event is just to exhort men and women to do something, to put into operation this spirit of goodwill. They regard it primarily as an occasion when one can be talking about war and peace, an occasion which we should use in order to plead with people to strive to put an end to war, to abolish armaments, and to get the nations to be friendly and so on.

So the prevailing opinion is divided into those two groups, and I call your attention, therefore, to this tremendous statement here in the Magnificat in order that we may see together how utterly and completely false all that is. If ever there was a subject that primarily needs *thought*, it is this whole question of the birth of the Son of God. That is why I preach this evening and do not have a Carol Service. You must think before you sing, otherwise your singing will be of no value. This is an occasion demanding sober, serious, vital thinking. There is no season of the year that the devil would so rob us of, in the way that I have indicated, as this particular season in connection with the birth of our blessed Lord.

Good News
So let us consider what we are told here about these fundamental principles concerning the nature of the gospel of our Lord and Saviour Jesus Christ. What is the real message of Christmas? The *first* thing that stands out, obviously, is this: *it is good news*; it is meant to be a proclamation. Everything

about it suggests that. Do you not remember the beginnings? If you read the whole of this first chapter of the Gospel according to St Luke, you will find that from the beginning it was like that. There is Zacharias, the father of John the Baptist, doing his duty, taking his turn, as it were, according to the course of the priests: doing his ordinary duty anticipating and expecting nothing. Suddenly, an angel appears to him. And the angel does not ask him to do something; he makes an announcement to him, telling him what God is going to do. Elisabeth, his wife, had been barren and they had agreed that they would never have any children; but the announcement is that she is going to bear a son, a child, who will be the forerunner of the Messiah who is about to come. That is how it begins.

And then in the case of Mary you get exactly the same thing. Here is the simple maiden, obviously anticipating nothing. Suddenly the archangel Gabriel appears to her, begins to address her, and says: 'Hail, *thou that art* highly favoured.' It is an announcement! And so it continues. And, even as Elisabeth has already done, Mary makes it perfectly clear in her song that she grasps this.

The gospel, my dear friends, is good news. It cannot be, therefore, primarily an exhortation; it is not some vague nebulous spirit; it is a mighty proclamation. You must think of this in terms of a town crier, in terms of an announcement made on the radio or anywhere else. That is the way to approach it. But the world does not approach it like that. It takes it, at the instigation of the devil, and twists it into something that belongs to its own philosophy. And it is a denial of this proclamation.

You can look at the Bible like this, let me put it in the modern form: you know how, from time to time, when something really remarkable is going to be announced, preliminary intimations are given that at such and such an hour a great statement, an announcement, is going to be made. We had it especially during the war[1] and it still happens in a sense. Hours before the thing happens we are told: 'Listen at such and such a time and you will hear something marvellous.' So we are all expectant and waiting and then comes the announcement.

Now, that is the kind of thing you find in the New Testament. In the Old Testament you have the preliminary announcements – that is the prophets. They began to say a long way back: 'Look, something is going to happen, God will do something.' So a proclamation, an announcement, was made, and everybody was waiting. Oh, the years had passed, many had forgotten, but at last it came. Good news! Proclamation. Announcement. Something that leads to rejoicing. And this stands out on the very surface of these preliminary portions in the Gospels.

God's Action
Secondly, it should surely be self-evident that this is something entirely of God. *It is an announcement*

1   The Second World War

of what God has done, is doing and will do. That is the essence of it all and it stands out in this Magnificat. God has done this. God will manifest his power. That is what Christmas is about. Not what men are going to do, nor what they should do. No, no – what God has done. We are asked to stand back and to look and listen. Everything in these early chapters should make us see that. Look at those shepherds. There they were in the field at night watching their flocks. They had done the same thing hundreds, thousands of times before; they were expecting nothing at all. Suddenly, they hear this singing, this announcement, and they are arrested by it and they look up. That is how Christmas comes.

You see, God has done something. Indeed, it is all of God. The gospel is a great record of God's mighty activity. It is the showing forth of his power. As Zacharias says subsequently so perfectly, the essence of the message is this: 'he hath visited and redeemed his people' (Luke 1:68).

And if we do not start with our thinking about Christmas in those terms, we are already wrong; we have gone astray. This is something that comes to us and should make us stand and look and lift up our heads and say: 'We are listening, what has God done?' That is it! God has done something; God's action; a manifestation of the right hand of God's power. So I want to emphasise the fact that it is entirely, exclusively of God.

Let me put it to you like this once more. The gospel is not, in the first instance, a call upon us to do anything at all. That is where this travesty of the gospel comes in: as if the whole message of Christmas was an appeal to us – 'Now then, be at your best during this season; let's make use of it; can't you conspire together and act together and try to get rid of war and bring in peace' – as if it were something primarily political; something we are going to do; a spirit that we must manifest and put into operation.

But it is not that at all! It is an announcement of one of the wonderful works of God. The whole Bible is a record of the activity of God: God creating; God coming down to man after he had fallen; God making a nation; God giving it kings; God sending prophets. 'But when the fulness of the time was come, God sent forth his Son, made of a woman, made under the law' (Gal. 4:4). The wonderful works of God! I protest in the name of the Bible, in the name of God, at this twisting, this perverting of the gospel into something which it is not! It is a proclamation and an announcement of what God has done in the person of his only begotten Son.

This becomes particularly clear and evident in these words of Mary. This is not only God's action, but it is a complete reversal of everything that people have ever thought or still think. Not only is this not a record of what men and women have done or are supposed to do, it is the exact opposite of all human thinking. It cuts right across it: it turns it upside down. And that is what I want to unfold to you now.

REVERSAL

The most surprising thing that has ever happened in this world is the coming of the Son of God into it. The most revolutionary thing in the world today is the Christian gospel. Why? Because it is the exact opposite almost of anything that you and I would ever have imagined or thought of.

God's Way

Let me show you what I mean. Look at it like this in the *first* place. *Look at the way in which God has done this thing.* That is what we are reminded of so forcibly in this particular section of the Magnificat. When God comes to take the action that is to save mankind, how does he do it? Who would ever have anticipated or imagined that he would do it by the birth of a helpless babe? But that is exactly how he did it. Who would have thought that when this babe was to be born, the woman selected would be some unknown nonentity, some ordinary poor handmaiden. You and I would not do it like that, would we? The world would not do it like that. We would not start by doing it through a babe. We would have somebody suddenly coming out of heaven: a great apparition, a great display. We are fond of drama, of propaganda; we are fond of doing things in a big way with a blowing of trumpets.

But that was not God's way. He did it like this. And, of course, if we had decided that it should happen through a babe like this, well, at least we would have chosen a queen, some great person, as the mother. When the Son of God comes into the world, why, it must be from the most dignified and most glorious person we can find. But it was a lowly handmaiden that nobody had ever heard of who was the one chosen by God.

So this is something that cuts across all our ideas, and then you notice something else. There are many points like this. I am simply glancing at one or two of them.

Look, secondly, where he was born. Where do you think the Son of God will be born when he comes into the world? I suppose it will be in the most marvellous, most fabulous palace that has ever been built or conceived of, costing millions, billions of pounds. All of gold and all of marble, everything that is wonderful.

No, no. He was born in a stable with the cattle by his side, and the straw and the manger. My dear friends, this is Christmas! Get rid of your human notions. Christmas is not the acme of human thinking; it is not an extension of all that man proposes to do. It is the exact opposite of it all. It is God! And the thing that is emphasised is the antithesis, the surprise, the amazement of it all.

Demolition

But come, let us look at it in more detail. Notice the way in which God's action for the salvation of man condemns and, indeed, demolishes all in which men and women trust or have ever trusted. Did you notice that? 'He hath shewed strength with his arm...' How? Well, '[H]e hath scattered ...' That is a very strong word; it means that he has scattered them completely until nothing is left. '[H]e hath scattered the proud in the imagination of their hearts. He hath put down the mighty ... and the rich he hath sent empty away.'

Is it not almost incredible that anybody could mis-read this gospel? It is not only a complete reversal of everything that man has ever proposed, it condemns, it demolishes, it scatters everything in which man by nature trusts.

HUMAN WISDOM

What are these things? *The first is his own wisdom.* It is important that we read the second half of verse 51 correctly: 'he hath scattered' – Who? – those who are 'proud in the imagination of their hearts'. And that means those who are haughty with respect to the reasoning or the understanding power of their hearts. The proud are those – and this is the meaning of the word that is used – who put themselves above others, the brainy people, the experts. The gospel of Jesus Christ, you see, is always contemporary. It was contemporary and up to date nearly two thousand years ago when it first came. It is equally contemporary today. There were haughty, proud people 'in the imagination of their hearts' then, and we still have them. The picture is of those who are very proud of their ability and their knowledge, their understanding, their brains, their capacity to think.

The world has always had many such people. You will find them described in the Old Testament and at the time when the Lord Jesus Christ came into the world; the world was even then full of them. Who were they? They were primarily the great Greek philosophers. There had been a mighty succession of them: Plato, Socrates, Aristotle and their schools of thinking, genius at its very highest, trying to understand life and proud of it. Proud of their learning, proud of their knowledge, proud of their understanding.

And what we are told here out of the mouth of Mary about the gospel and its effect is this: that the coming of the Son of God into the world scatters them. Dismisses them. Demolishes them. And it does so completely. How does it do so? Fortunately we have many answers to that question in the New Testament itself. Our Lord himself supplied one notable answer. You will find it at the end of the eleventh chapter of the Gospel according to St Matthew. He said, 'I thank thee, O Father, Lord of heaven and earth, because thou hast hid these things from the wise and prudent, and hast revealed them unto babes. Even so, Father: for so it seemed good in thy sight' (Matt. 11:25, 26).

He means this: he says in effect, 'It's obvious that the wise and prudent, the philosophers, the teachers, the great men, the great intellects are confounded by me; they are confused by me; they are questioning me, trying to catch me, trying to trap me. They are not believing in me; they are remaining where they were, and it is the babes, the ignoramuses, as it were, who are crowding into the kingdom.'

It was hid from the wise and prudent; they were made to look foolish. The great minds, the great brains, were left where they were. But it does not even stop at that; it goes further. The apostle Paul has a very interesting commentary on this. Indeed, it is obvious, is it not, that in this Magnificat we have, in a kind of nutshell, what is the very essence of the gospel as worked out in greater detail by our Lord himself, and by his servant, the apostle Paul. Paul puts it like this: '... the world by wisdom knew not God', and when the world by wisdom, by philosophy, by reason and understanding failed to arrive at God, '... it pleased God by the foolishness of preaching to save them that believe. For the Jews require a sign, and the Greeks seek after wisdom' (1 Cor. 1:21, 22).

Those are the people who are seeking after wisdom – the 'proud in the imagination of their hearts'. The people who are proud in their intellect, their knowledge, their science, their understanding. These are men and women who can give a rational explanation. They pit their minds against it all. And what we are told is that the effect of the coming of the Son of God into the world scatters them, dismisses them, makes them look silly. And it is still doing so.

There has never, perhaps, been a time in the long history of the human race when the philosophers have been made to look quite so silly as they are today. It is the philosophers and scientists and others who have been teaching us, for a hundred years and more, that man is evolving and developing and advancing, and that by his own efforts he can make a perfect world. They have believed it, and they have been preaching it and driving it home to us, and yet the whole world is making them look utterly ridiculous. They have been 'scattered ... in the imagination of their hearts'.

Yes, but there is something that scatters them more than contemporary history does, and that is this message concerning Christmas. It does it like this: this is the final proof of their failure to find God. Do you listen to them sometimes on these programmes – *Brains Trust, Any Questions* and so on? Do you hear them talking their folly about immortality and about various other things? How foolish they seem. They do not know, you see. They have no knowledge, no understanding. They have been trying to understand the mystery, and they cannot, of course. They have failed completely. They have their ideas about God but they are not satisfied. How can they be? How can they define God? How can a man with a finite mind encompass the eternal, the infinite and the absolute? They are made to look silly, are they not? And that is exactly what Mary says: 'he hath scattered the proud in the imagination of their hearts.'

'The world by wisdom knew not God.' Do not misunderstand me. I am not here to denounce intellect. I am not here to denounce ability. I am not here even to denounce philosophy. But what I am here to denounce is pride of intellect, pride of knowledge, pride of understanding. The attitude of the modern man who says: 'I am sufficient and complete. God?' he says, 'Very well then, put him on the table, let me examine him, I'll tell you what I think about God.' That is what I am denouncing, and that is what the coming of Christ scatters, makes it look idiotic because, with all their wisdom and ability and learning, men and women have not arrived at God. They have failed completely. They never get further than saying 'What if? Perhaps. Perchance. It is possible' – and no more. 'The world by wisdom knew not God.'

Our Lord exposes that. But he does not stop at doing it like that, of course. '[T]he proud in the imagination of their hearts' are scattered in another way: *when the true wisdom confronted them, they could not see it.* The apostle Paul is very eloquent on this. This is where the intellectually proud have been made to look ridiculous. They say they are men and women of wisdom and that when they see the truth they will grasp it. They like to call themselves 'seekers after truth'. But if you call yourself a seeker after truth you are denying the gospel.

Truth can never be found by you, or by another person. Truth is revealed. But here are the seekers after truth. They say: 'We want nothing but truth. Give us truth; show us truth; help us to arrive at truth; it's all we want.' Suddenly, truth stands before them in the person of a man, and they do not recognise him. The apostle Paul puts it like this: 'Which none of the princes of this world knew: for had they known *it*, they would not have crucified the Lord of glory' (1 Cor. 2:8). 'Monstrous!' they said. 'Son of God, a carpenter? Ridiculous! Son of God, an ignoramus, an artisan? Impossible! Wisdom must always be in a philosopher, must belong to the schools. Who is this fellow?' They ridiculed him.

'For the Jews require a sign, and the Greeks seek after wisdom: But we preach Christ crucified, unto the Jews a stumblingblock, and unto the Greeks foolishness' (1 Cor. 1:22-23). And by saying that it was foolishness, they were displaying their own folly. They did not recognise truth when it was standing incarnate before their eyes.

So Mary is perfectly right. '[H]e hath scattered the proud in the imagination of their hearts...' And, as I have already said, the gospel does it supremely, of course, by the way in which God chose to do it. When he chose to send wisdom to men, he sent it thus in the form of a babe and a carpenter, an ordinary man, as it were. And so, what the Greeks and the wise and the proud of intellect have been totally and utterly incapable of doing, God does in this extraordinary manner. And the wise and the proud are the laughing stock of the universe at this moment. They are the people, above all others, who, in their pride of intellect, are rejecting God's wisdom, God's power, God's way of salvation. He does indeed scatter the proud in the imagination of their hearts.

PRIDE

Secondly, 'He hath put down the mighty from their seats' (emphasis added). This is a great theme in the Bible. God is always doing this. He knows that the final sin in the hearts of men and women is the sin of pride. They are proud of intellect, proud of position, proud of power, proud of status; and so God is always fighting it, and demolishing it, always throwing it down. Look at how he has done this in the whole case of the nation of the Jews. There were the nations of the world, proud of their might and their prowess and their armies. But God made a nation for himself out of one man called Abraham; and a very weak nation it was, with just a little country – Palestine. What a small bit of earth it was, his little nation amidst the mighty dynasties of Assyria, Babylon and Ninevah, and all the rest of them! But that is God's way. And he was always ridiculing and bringing down these mighty ones, through his own people.

You see it typified to perfection in the great story about David and Goliath. Here is the mighty, on his seat, the Goliath, the great power that is irresistible and is threatening to demolish the whole world. And a stripling of a lad comes along who does not have a sword and who has no armour; he only has a sling and five stones. And he just flings one of them, strikes Goliath's forehead and brings to earth, demolishes that mighty tyrant.

And that is God's way of dealing with the world. That is what God has always been doing. That is what he is doing in his Son. He does not send a great chieftain, a great prince; he sends a babe. And so it has continued. Look at it in the case of a man like Nebuchadnezzar. He had conquered so much and he was so wealthy; he set himself up as a god and told people to worship him. And do you know what happened to him? If you look at him in a few months, you will find him like an ox eating grass in a field; his nails had grown like talons, hair had covered his body and the dew fell upon him. A maniac, a raving maniac! What was happening? O, God was 'put[ting] down the mighty from *their* seats.'

But he has done it finally in a supreme manner. When the King of kings and the Lord of lords came into this world, he came into a stable. If you do not feel a sense of holy laughter within you, I do not see that you have a right to think that you are a Christian. Thank God, this is the gospel, this is salvation. God turning upside down, reversing everything we have ever thought, everything we have taken pride in. The mighty? Why, he will pull them down from their seats. He has been doing so. He is still doing so. Let any man arise and say he is going to govern, to be the god of the whole world; you need not be afraid – he will be put down. Every dictator has gone down; they all do. Finally, the devil and all that belong to him will go down to the lake of fire and will be destroyed forever. The Son of God has come into the world to do that.

Empty

But then, *thirdly*, *'the rich'*, we are told, *'he hath sent empty away'* (emphasis added). This is not to be taken in a material sense primarily, but in a moral sense. What is the effect of the coming of the Son of God into this world? It is to send the rich away empty. That is the great story that I see in the four Gospels. Look at it in the rich young ruler. There was a rich man, rich in money. Yes, but priding himself on his richness in morality, he said: 'All these [commandments] have I kept from my youth up' (Luke 18:21). How rich he was in morals, in ethics and in righteousness. But when he stood before this Son of God, this babe of Bethlehem, who had become a man and was beginning to teach at the age of thirty, when the rich young ruler, who had kept the commandments of God and was full and overflowing with righteousness, looks into the face of the Son of God, he listens to his words, and what is the end of the story? He went away sorrowful. He came with pride; he went away sorrowful. His riches were made to look very tawdry.

But he is only one of many instances. This was the whole trouble with the Pharisees and that is why they hated our Lord. That is why they finally conspired to crucify and to kill him. The effect of the coming of the Son of God upon the Pharisees was to send them empty away. And they were so rich! But when they listened to the preaching of the Son of God, they could see their righteousness disappearing: all they had boasted of, all they had gloated in, all they had prided themselves on; their exceptional righteousness, they who had never committed adultery. 'Wait a minute,' says the Son of God, 'have you ever looked on a woman to lust? If you have, you have committed adultery with her, in your heart. That is what matters.' And their righteousness had gone. They were all guilty. They thought they were innocent. They were not!

He took them through point by point in the Sermon on the Mount. He showed them the spiritual character of God's law. And these men, who thought they had kept the law of God to perfection, found themselves guilty on every point. And they hated him. Why? He sent them away empty. They thought they were rich.

This is what he has always done. Men and women are very satisfied with themselves and their own lives until they look into the face of Jesus Christ. But the moment they look at him and listen to his interpretation of God's law, they begin to say that 'There is none righteous, no, not one' (Rom. 3:10).

A man says: 'I'm a good fellow, I've got my code, I'm better than this man, I am much better than that one, I do a lot of good, I'm wonderful' – as the Pharisee said it in the temple (Luke 18:11). And then he finds that God's law is that, 'Thou shalt love the Lord thy God with all thy heart, and with all thy soul, and with all thy strength, and with all thy mind; and thy neighbour as thyself' (Luke 10:27). And he has not started, he is nowhere. He listens to Christ saying: 'Blessed *are* the poor in spirit' (Matt. 5:3), and he is so full of pride, he is damned already, and he goes away empty. 'Blessed *are* the meek' (Matt. 5:5), and he is the opposite to meekness. 'Blessed *are* they which do hunger and thirst after righteousness' (Matt. 5:6), and he is boasting of his righteousness. He is sent empty away.

O, this Son of God always sends the rich empty away. Really to know him and to understand his teaching brings men and women to see that the whole world lies guilty before God. 'For all have sinned, and come short of the glory of God' (Rom. 3:23). Every one of us, the best of us. Our righteousness is but as filthy rags.

But see it supremely in the case of that great man the apostle Paul, when he was Saul of Tarsus. What a wonderful man he was! Israelite of the Israelites, Hebrew of the Hebrews, of the tribe of Benjamin and so on; knowing the Lord God better than most other people. Yet, he suddenly met Christ, and the wealth he boasted of, the riches in which he gloated became manure, refuse, vile. 'I ... do count them *but* dung' (Phil. 3:8). It was hopeless. He had gone away empty. He was nothing. He had been stripped, he was naked. 'I was alive', he says, 'without the law once: but when the commandment came, sin revived, and I died' (Rom. 7:9). He had nothing at all. The rich are sent empty away.

And so it is right through the Gospels. Mary has seen it. She has had a glimpse, a flash of it. He always does these things. Can you not see that everything that man boasts in, his intellect, his understanding, his power, his social status, his influence, his righteousness, his morality, his ethics, his code – every one of them is utterly demolished by this Son of God.

GOD'S BLESSING
This is the exact opposite of everything man thinks and boasts of.

People
You see it, firstly, in the people whom he blesses. Who are those who are to be blessed? The answer is, 'the babes', 'them who are of low degree'. 'For ye see your calling, brethren,' says Paul to the Corinthians, 'how that not many wise men ... not many mighty, not many noble, *are called* ... and God hath chosen the weak things of the world to confound the things which are mighty; And base things ... and things which are not, to bring to nought things that are: That no flesh should glory in his presence' (1 Cor. 1:26-29).

Who are the blessed? Here they are: 'Blessed *are* they which do hunger and thirst after righteousness'. 'Blessed *are* the poor in spirit.' 'Blessed *are* they that mourn...' 'Blessed *are* the meek' (Matt. 5:1-12). These are the people. The nobodies. He blesses them. The world does not look at it like that. It is the great; it is the influential, it is the able, it is the wonderful. No, no. God is acting and God does it in entire reverse.

Way
But notice, *secondly, the way in which he gives the blessing*. And this is the special glory of this Christmas message. '[T]he world by wisdom knew not God' (1 Cor. 1:21), but suddenly God sends his wisdom and his revelation. These things men and women cannot arrive at by searching. 'But God hath revealed *them* unto us by his Spirit: for the Spirit searcheth all things, yea, the deep things of God' (1 Cor. 2:10). We have the mind of Christ. We are made wise. Here is a way whereby a man or woman can know God. What Plato, Socrates, Aristotle and all the succession of mighty secular philosophers have failed to find is given as a free gift to the babes – those who admit that they cannot find it.

Those who believe on the Lord Jesus Christ have a knowledge of God. They have an understanding of life, an understanding of themselves which the ablest, wisest people in the world, in a natural sense, entirely lack. Listen to them. I know of no better preparation for the preaching of the gospel than to ask people to listen to Bertrand Russell, and Julian Huxley, and the rest. Ask them for an explanation of man and of life and of death and of God, and they have nothing to tell you. They do not know! They are completely bankrupt.

The simplest and most ignorant Christian has a knowledge and an understanding that is completely denied to such people. 'I thank thee, O Father, Lord of heaven and earth, because thou hast hid these things from the wise and prudent, and hast revealed them unto babes. Even so, Father: for so it seemed good in thy sight' (Matt. 11:25-26). The people who are wisest in the world are these simple Christian people. They are not afraid of tomorrow. They are not afraid of death. They know they are in the right relationship to God. They are not surprised that the world is as it is. It is the great men who are surprised. 'But', they say, 'we cannot understand it; this is the twentieth century; we are more learned, and we are meeting one another, and we are having conferences; why is the world as it is?' And they do not understand it. Why? Because they know nothing about sin. It is in them. They are full of it, but they do not understand it. They do not have the wisdom that God gives, the revelation that has come in Christ.

Exaltation

Then, *look at the way in which he exalts us.* 'He hath put down the mighty from their seats' and, on the other hand, 'exalted them of low degree'. It does not matter who you are or what you are as a Christian, if you are a Christian, you are a child of God. You will not appear in the New Year's Honours List – they have never heard of you, and *The Times* knows nothing about you; but, thank God, you are in the Court Circular of heaven, children of God, members of the heavenly royal family. He has made us, says John, 'kings and priests unto God' (Rev. 1:6). Or, if you prefer it, a kingdom of priests, children of God, 'heirs of God, and joint-heirs with Christ' (Rom. 8:17). Exalted us!

'Blessed *are* the meek: for they shall inherit the earth.' You are not in any great man's will. It is all right. You are a poor person, you are an ignoramus, the world does not know of you; but if you are a Christian you are in God's will. You are in the will of God and you are a joint-heir with Christ, and you are going to enter into that inheritance with him. You will reign with him. You will judge the world, you will judge angels with the Son of God. Here is the exaltation: 'He hath put down the mighty from their seats, and exalted them of low degree.' Blessed be the name of God!

Filled

And *lastly*, what a phrase this is: 'He hath filled the hungry with good things.' 'Blessed *are* they which do hunger and thirst after righteousness...' Why? O, 'they shall be filled' (Matt. 5:6)! 'The rich he hath sent empty away.' We have seen that. But look at the opposite: the hungry, the man who feels he is a sinner, vile. The man who feels he is a cad, the man who cannot understand himself. The man who feels he is rotten. The man who says to himself, 'in me (that is, in my flesh), dwelleth no good thing' (Rom. 7:18). The man who says, 'O wretched man that I am! Who shall deliver me from the body of this death?' (Rom. 7:24). The man who says 'Everything I do is wrong; it's tarnished, it's sinful; my best actions are ignoble. There is nothing right about me at all. I hate myself. I cannot deliver myself. What can be done with such a wretch as I am?'

What about him? He shall be 'filled with good things'. What are they? Well, righteousness: he is hungering and thirsting after righteousness. He is poor in spirit, he is mourning because of his sinfulness and the sins he has committed. He does not know what to do. Blessed is such a man, says Christ. He shall be filled with righteousness. It means that God sent his Son into this world in order that we might be made righteous. We cannot make ourselves righteous. The whole world has failed. Men and women in their blind manner try to seek it in a sense, but they cannot. They are wrong in their very notions. But suddenly they are awakened and convicted; they want it. Suddenly, they are given it. It is all in Christ. 'Christ *is* the end of the law for righteousness to every one that believeth' (Rom. 10:4).

Now this sounds incredible. That is why people do not believe it. But this is the gospel. Do you know it means this: here I am, born in sin, shapen in iniquity. I myself have sinned. My nature is vile and rotten. I am a hopeless mass of perdition. What does the gospel tell me? It tells me that if I believe in the Lord Jesus Christ truly and trust myself to him, then his righteousness is upon me; my sins are blotted out as if I had never committed a single sin in my life. God pronounces me to be righteous. He has put to my account the righteousness of Christ. I am a pauper; my books are empty; I am damned; I am doomed. Suddenly, the wealth of the Son of God is put into my account. 'He hath filled' – filled! – 'the hungry with good things...'

So the message of Christmas is this: that whatever you are – you may, until now, have been a pauper in rags in a spiritual and in a moral sense – but you can be filled with good things, clothed with the righteousness of Christ, filled with a sense of peace towards God. Peace in your breast. No longer afraid of death; no longer afraid of the grave; no longer afraid of the judgement. Filled with peace within and towards God. Contentment!

> Content to let the world go by,
> To know no pain nor loss –
> My sinful self my only shame,
> My glory all – the cross.
>
> Elizabeth Cecilia Clephane (1830-69)

CHRISTMAS GIFT

What a Christmas gift! That is what is offered. The gospel is not just an exhortation to you to join a peace society, or to start organising for peace in industry, or here or there. You may do that later, but have you started here? Are you filled? Are you filled with a knowledge of God? Are you filled with the righteousness of Christ? Have you got peace in your heart? Have you lost the fear of life and death, and the grave and judgement and hell? Have you the joy of the Lord? Are you able to rejoice even in tribulations and in spite of circumstance and accident and chance? 'He hath filled the hungry with good things...' Related to the Father eternal, the giver of every good and every perfect gift: his children, his heirs. Is not contentment a wonderful thing? Not forever striving at what you cannot get, seeking what will never come to you, but a satisfaction. '[B]eing justified by faith, we have peace with God through our Lord Jesus Christ: By whom also we have access by faith into this grace wherein we stand ...' (Rom. 5:1-2). Access to God as Father, the eternal giver, with no end to his largesse and his capacity to bless. And more, we 'rejoice in hope of the glory of God' (Rom. 5:2). The hungry he hath filled with good things: the fruit of the Spirit, love, peace, long-suffering, goodness, meekness, temperance, faith – filled with them! O, says Paul to the Ephesians, I am praying for you that you may be 'filled with all the fulness of God', that the love of Christ may come into your hearts; that you may know its 'breadth, and length, and depth, and height', and may 'know the love of Christ, which passeth knowledge, that ye might be filled with all the fulness of God' (Eph. 3:17-19).

That is the message of salvation. That is the good news of the gospel. Mary saw it in a flash. She spoke it. She uttered it. This is the gospel. What God has done. What God will offer. 'This one who will be born out of me,' says Mary, 'I don't understand it, but he is going to be the benefactor of mankind. That's what he is going to give. He will reverse everything. He will bring down the intellectually proud, the mighty men, the self-satisfied, the morally rich. But the common people will hear him gladly. He will give us a wisdom, a knowledge and an understanding that will baffle us to all eternity. He will make us children of God and joint-heirs with himself. He will fill us even with himself, and finally with glory.

Beloved friends, beloved people, have you heard this message? Are you surprised now that the angels sang, that everybody sings, when they really know who he is and why he came into this world? Are you too wise for these things? If you are, you have nothing to look forward to but to be scattered. Are you too big, too great to humble yourself? You will be brought down. You will lie on your deathbed in helplessness and hopelessness, in despair, realising that you have nothing.

Are you rich? The day will come when you will realise that you are empty-handed and have nothing at all. So humble yourself. See your need. Believe on the Lord Jesus Christ, the babe of Bethlehem, the Christ of Calvary, the glorious One that rose in the resurrection, the King of Kings, the Lord of Lords, seated at the right hand of God at this minute. The King who is coming back to reign. Fall at his feet. Believe in him. Give yourself to him, and he will fill you until you are overflowing with his own glorious riches.

3

THE FAITHFULNESS OF GOD

'He hath helped his servant Israel, in remembrance of *his* mercy; As he spake to our fathers, to Abraham, and to his seed for ever' (Luke 1:54-55).

First of all, we must correct the Authorised (King James) Version at this point. The first phrase in verse 55 – 'As he spake to our fathers' – should really be in brackets. So we read like this: 'He hath holpen his servant Israel in remembrance of his mercy to Abraham and to his seed for ever (as he spake to our fathers).' The correction is important for this reason only, that the Authorised translation gives the impression that the reference to

Abraham and to his seed is a continuation of the speaking to the fathers. That is, in a sense, perfectly true, as we shall see, but the main idea is better expressed by the other rendering.

So we come back to a further consideration of the Magnificat, this extraordinary statement spoken or sung by the virgin Mary after she had been greeted by Elisabeth, the mother of John the Baptist. It is, as we have indicated, a most astonishing utterance, particularly when you look at it from the standpoint of seeing in it a summary of the salient and basic features of the Christian message, the Christian gospel, the Christian faith.

We have considered how Mary seems to see that the thing that overshadows everything else is the manifestation of the character of God in the coming of his Son into this world. And we saw, too, how she goes on to indicate how some of the attributes of God's person and character have been made manifest and bare before us in the great event and fact of the Incarnation; so with the whole of her being, her soul and spirit, she praises God and magnifies his great and holy name.

Then we saw in a striking manner how Mary here immediately realises that the gospel is a reversal of everything that man would ever have thought of. We saw how in the Gospels things happen which are not only inconceivable to man but are also the exact opposite of what man would ever imagine God would do. This is what he has done. '[H]e that is mighty hath done to me great things; and holy *is* his name' (v. 49). 'He hath shewed strength with his arm; he hath scattered' – who? – 'the proud in the imagination of their hearts. He hath put down the mighty from *their* seats, and exalted them of low degree' (vv. 51, 52).

That is the great characteristic of the gospel. Thank God for it! 'Not the righteous; sinners Jesus came to save.' 'They that are whole', he says, 'have no need of the physician, but they that are sick: I came not to call the righteous [the wealthy in this respect], but sinners to repentance' (Mark 2:17). O, thank God that the gospel, in a sense, starts with these words: 'Blessed *are* the poor in spirit ... Blessed *are* they that mourn ... Blessed *are* the meek ... Blessed *are* they which do hunger and thirst after righteousness' (Matt. 5:3-6). And Mary has anticipated all that; this Magnificat is a synopsis of the Sermon on the Mount in a sense, especially the Beatitudes.

So we have been looking at those aspects of her great statement, and it is indeed thus full, pregnant with a setting forth of the great central features of this gospel of redemption. But we come back now to a further consideration of it, especially these two verses, because here we are reminded of something in connection with what happened when the Son of God came into this world, which is, in many ways, one of the most comforting aspects of the faith and of the whole of the biblical teaching.

FULFILLED PROPHECY

That aspect is simply this: the Incarnation is the supreme example of fulfilled prophecy, the supreme example of God's faithfulness to his promises. And this is surely most comforting, especially as we consider it in the setting of the world in which we find ourselves.

We all agree that these are no easy days for Christians. Indeed they are exceptionally difficult days for the whole of the Christian Church. Contrast it with what one reads of in the nineteenth century, when it was the custom for people to go to places of worship, and when everybody thought in such terms. What a change has taken place! So many Christian people are discouraged. Therefore, what can we do better on a last Sunday morning of an old year (27 December 1959) than to look at the situation in which we find ourselves in the light of this message of the Incarnation, the message of Christmas, and to see what, over and above the great fact itself, it has to say to us in this more general manner. And here, as I see it, there are some three principles which stand out with exceptional clarity.

Fulfilment of God's Promises

The *first* is that the coming of Christ into this world is *the fulfilment of all of God's promises*. That is what Mary is really saying: 'He hath holpen his servant Israel, in remembrance of *his* mercy ... to Abraham, and to his seed for ever.' Now the great covenant promise concerning redemption was, after all, made in its most explicit manner to Abraham. You can find it prior to that, but the definition of it, as it were, the explicit statement of it, is made to Abraham when he is told that in him, in his seed, shall all the world be blessed (Gen. 13:15).

And Mary at once sees the significance of what is happening – the Son that is to be born out of her womb. She remembers what the archangel Gabriel said about him; she did not understand it then, but now she does, and she begins to realise the meaning of 'He shall be great, and shall be called the Son of the Highest' (Luke 1:32). She begins to understand what Elisabeth means when she says: 'Blessed *art* thou among women, and blessed *is* the fruit of thy womb. And whence *is* this to me, that the mother of my Lord should come to me' (Luke 1:42-43).

Mary here sees that now God is going to fulfil all these promises that he has made. This 'mercy toward Abraham and his seed for ever'. But how is it happening? 'It happens', she says, 'like this, "He hath *holpen* his servant Israel,"' and that word means to succour, to help, or, perhaps better still, to lift up. Israel had been cast down; they need to be lifted up, they need to be saved. They had been thrown down by an enemy but someone comes, rescues them, takes hold of them and puts them to stand upon their feet. So she says in effect: 'When I give birth to the Son, I am giving birth to the

Saviour; the one prophesied, predicted, promised. He is coming. All that was promised to Abraham, all this great mercy, here it is, literally coming into being and into action.' She is referring primarily, of course, to salvation itself, and this is where her statement is so significant. God had made this promise to Abraham concerning salvation, forgiveness of sins and reconciliation unto himself. And what we so often tend to forget is that what God said to Abraham was that this salvation that was to come was to be brought about through this descendant of his that was yet to be born into this world. Now Abraham did not understand it fully; but he understood enough to rest his faith upon it. '[H]e [Abraham] believed in the LORD; and he counted it to him for righteousness' (Gen. 15:6).

Paul takes it up and works it out as a great argument in the fourth chapter of his Epistle to the Romans, and also in the third chapter of the Epistle to the Galatians. Our Lord himself also said to the Jews on one occasion: 'Your father Abraham rejoiced to see my day: and he saw *it,* and was glad' (John 8:56). Now that is a reference to salvation. That is a statement which means that Abraham was given to see, in a flash – not very clearly, but he saw it – that God's great salvation, the forgiveness of sins and reconciliation was to be brought about ultimately by someone who should come into the world, who would be of his seed.

Now Mary is making a very basic statement here. She sees it. 'That', she says, 'is what is happening.'

In other words, we have here a summary of the whole of the Old Testament, and nothing is more important than for us to realise that the whole of the Old Testament is looking forward to this event. The children of Israel were greatly blessed. They were God's own people. They were unlike all the other peoples and nations of the world, and God showered his blessings upon them.

But let us never make the mistake of imagining that they had had everything. All they ultimately had was the promise. It was enough. Thank God it was enough. But they had nothing more than that. You will find that this is frequently elaborated in the New Testament. There is that tremendous statement of it in Galatians 3; but you find it again in a very striking manner in the Epistle to the Hebrews, at the end of that great eleventh chapter: 'And these all, having obtained a good report through faith, received not the promise: God having provided some better thing for us, that they without us should not be made perfect' (Heb. 11:39-40). They did not receive the promise. What they received was the promise of the promise, the certainty that the promise would be fulfilled.

And here is the key, of course, to the understanding of the Old Testament. Look at those people as they went to their tabernacle and to their temple taking their burnt offerings and meal offerings and sacrifices: animals being killed, blood being shed, and offered, placed before the altar, and so on.

What is it all about? What was happening there? Well, the answer is that that was but a covering, as it were, of their sins for the time being. The argument is developed in the tenth chapter of the Hebrews: 'For *it is* not possible that the blood of bulls and of goats should take away sins' (Heb. 10:4). No, no! they were simply covered over. They were but types pointing to the coming of the great anti-type; they did not really deal with sin.

But they were indications that God had a way of dealing with sin, and that, says Mary, is what is now happening. Here are the mercies promised. God had given this promise that to Abraham and to his seed there would be mercy and compassion. Their sins should be forgiven and blotted out as a thick cloud; they would be made the children of God and heirs of glory, and all that they knew by way of offerings and sacrifices was not the fulfilment of that. It was merely another way of giving the promise and of indicating in a measure the way in which it was going to be fulfilled.

But here, now, says Mary, is the great antitype himself. Here now God is going to fulfil all this mercy that he had promised to Abraham and to his seed forever. And this means that there is only one way of salvation; it means that all salvation and every aspect of it comes in this one way – in Jesus Christ, the Son of God and him crucified, made an offering for sin. '[A] body hast thou prepared me' (Heb. 10:5) – what for? – in order that he might be the Lamb of God, that he might be slain, that he might be offered. One sacrifice forever. '[T]he Lamb of God, which taketh away the sin of the world' (John 1:29).

That is what Mary is saying. Here is the fulfilment of all the mercies. There is no forgiveness apart from Jesus Christ and him crucified. There is no true knowledge of God apart from him. There is no blessing apart from him – as the apostle Paul puts it in 2 Corinthians 1:20: 'For all the promises of God in him are yea, and in him Amen, unto the glory of God by us.' 'He hath holpen his servant Israel...' Here is Israel, seed of Abraham. Yes, but under the law and condemned by the law. Not able to be free; held in bondage and in captivity; living on the promises, thank God, but nothing more.

Here is the great fulfilment; and so you will find that all the Old Testament prophets, psalmists, seers have seen this. They are looking forward; they know that this is what will fulfil all the promises and bring the mercy into the individual experience. It is all in and through our Lord and Saviour Jesus Christ and what he did when he was in this world, and what he is now continuing and applying in the glory.

Blessing for the World
That is the first aspect. But there is a *second* aspect to this general statement, that the Incarnation is the supreme example of fulfilled prophecy, for there was also this other promise made to Abraham that in him and his seed all the world

should be blessed. Not only in the sense I have just been describing, but in addition to that. And this is the point at which the Jews, the children of Israel of old, stumbled so sadly. They did not realise that God was promising to Abraham that not only they, the literal, physical seed, should be blessed but that all the nations of the earth should be blessed through this person, 'not of the Jews only, but also of the Gentiles' (Rom. 9:24).

This is the key to the understanding of the Epistle to the Romans. The Jews thought that this salvation was only for them. They stumbled at our Lord when he said that he was not come only for the lost sheep of the House of Israel, and gave indications of something further. They always stumbled at this – that salvation was to come to the Gentiles. But here is the promise made to Abraham, and Mary is given the insight to see it, and she glories in this fact. Here is one who is the Saviour of the world and, of course, he knew it himself. That is the explanation of the incident in John 12, when the Greeks approached Andrew and said: 'We would see Jesus.' Our Lord would not see them at the time but he said: 'And I, if I be lifted up from the earth, will draw all *men* unto me' (John 12:32). He means all nations, that his salvation is not confined to the Jews but is also for the Gentiles.

Peter stumbled at it and he was given a vision in connection with the visit of Cornelius. Here is the message: 'What God hath cleansed, *that* call not thou common' (Acts 10:15). The door is open to the Gentiles also. You and I would never have been Christians but for this – 'Abraham and his seed'. Who are Abraham's seed? O, not merely those who are of the circumcision, but of the uncircumcision also. All who have the faith of Abraham. Abraham is the father of all the faithful.

Abraham is the father of all who exercise faith in God through our Lord and Saviour Jesus Christ. Thank God that if we are Christians we are of the seed of Abraham. That is the argument of Galatians 3. And Mary puts it all here in a nutshell, as it were. 'He hath holpen his servant Israel, in remembrance of *his* mercy ... to Abraham, and to his seed for ever.' And it is all entirely and exclusively in and through our Lord and Saviour Jesus Christ.

Are we all quite happy and perfectly clear about this? You do not know God apart from Jesus Christ. You are not reconciled to God apart from him. It is in him that God has 'holpen his servant Israel'. It is here he fulfils all the gracious promises made to Abraham and to his seed for-ever. There is only one way to God: it is in Jesus Christ and him crucified. He said: 'I am the way, the truth, and the life: no man cometh unto the Father, but by me' (John 14:6). There is only one way to enter with boldness into the holiest of all. It is, as we are reminded in Hebrews 10:19, 'by the blood of Jesus'. Mary is expressing all that.

Method
Secondly, the Incarnation shows us *the method or the manner of God's blessing*. The coming of Christ, I have said, is the fulfilment of all God's promises. Yes, but let us observe the way in which he does it. The coming of Christ sheds this great illumination upon God's method, God's manner of fulfilling his own promises and bringing his mercies into being.

And the key to this is in the expression: *In remembrance* – 'He hath holpen his servant Israel, *in remembrance* [emphasis added] of *his* mercy ... to Abraham, and to his seed for ever. As he spake to our fathers'. Here again is a summary of the whole of the Old Testament. But now let us take this phrase *in remembrance*. Here is the comfort and the consolation of the Scripture.

'What is happening?' Mary seems to be saying to herself. 'Ah,' she says, 'what is happening is this: God, after all, has remembered his promise. In remembrance of his promise, of his mercies, of all he had said to Abraham and to the fathers through the running centuries.'

DOES GOD FORGET?
What she is saying, in effect, *first of all*, is this: *God seems to forget*, doesn't he? He seems to forget what he has promised. Yes, he has promised mercy to Abraham. When did he give that promise? And the startling answer is that he had given that promise to Abraham two thousand long years before Mary was singing these words. Two thousand years!

That is God's method. He calls Abraham one night and says: 'Come out of your tent; stand here, look at the stars in the heavens; can you count them? Imagine that you are looking at the sand on the sea-shore: can you count the individual granules?' 'So shall thy seed be'; 'in thee shall all families of the earth be blessed' (Gen. 12:3; 15:5). And then two thousand years elapse and the Messiah does not come. Has God forgotten his promise? Is there any value in his promise?

And here, you see, is the lesson; here is the comfort and the consolation. There is nothing that is quite so foolish as to judge God in terms of our time measurements and our calendars. There are so many discouraged Christian people in churches today. 'Ah,' they say, 'perhaps the higher critics are right after all. They say that there is no such thing as prophecy, that you cannot foretell, and that all the things we have spoken about the promises of God are nonsense. Christianity is nothing but a bit of ethics and morality which we must put into practice.' People are discouraged and ask whether it is true after all. 'Where are these promises of God? You who believe in them still, why are they not being fulfilled? Why does God allow this and that?'

Is that not the foolish talk and argument? Well, nobody who has heard these words of the Magnificat should ever say that again: 'in remembrance'. 'What is happening now', Mary says, 'is that God is fulfilling what he promised two thousand years ago.' Shame on us Christian people for thinking so much as worldings, and using the foolish methods of philosophy when we are dealing with the everlasting and eternal God. *In remembrance.* '[O]ne day *is* with the Lord as a thousand years, and a thousand years as one day' (2 Pet. 3:8). You will find the Psalmist crying out in his moment of almost despair and saying: 'Hath God forgotten to be gracious?' (Ps. 77:9). Of course he has not! It is he who does not know his Scriptures. He does not know his God. '[I]n remembrance', after two thousand years!

Yes, but let me add to that: not only had God made this promise two thousand years before, and all the years and centuries had passed and he had not come; there was something even more depressing than that. At the time when Mary uttered these words, there had been no prophetic word to Israel for four hundred years. The last of the prophets was Malachi and four hundred years had gone since Malachi had exercised his ministry. Can you imagine that? We who get so impatient if God does not answer us at once! Four hundred years and his chosen people had not had a single word. What is happening? 'Oh,' says Mary, 'what is happening is this: God is still there and God still remembers.'

That, then, is our first principle. We have all known something about this in personal experience, have we not? So let us learn this lesson – God never forgets, he cannot forget! He sees the end from the beginning; he is in the eternal now. He is from everlasting to everlasting. He is not in the flux of time; he is outside it. He does not see things as we do. He seems to forget but he does not. So the next time you are tempted to think that he does, you simply look at the fact of the Incarnation and it is the eternal answer to your fears.

Apparent Defeats

But the second point which emerges here is this: he not only seems to forget but *he also allows, apparently, defeats to take place even to his own people.* He called Abraham out of Ur of the Chaldees and he made his great statement and promise to him; he created a nation out of him, and blessed this nation. Yes, but look on a few years and you will find that that nation is in the captivity and bondage of Egypt. Look at the taskmasters and their whips; see the people bleeding and groaning under the dictatorship of Pharaoh. God allowed all that. They seemed to be utterly forsaken, defeated, and quite forlorn and without any hope at all. Look at it again in the case of the captivity of Babylon. It is the same thing: the city destroyed; the city of God reduced to a mass of rubble and ruins, with all the gorgeous buildings razed to the ground; the people carried out, taken away as slaves in utter helplessness into the captivity of Babylon.

God allowed all that. The God who had promised so much allowed all that. He allowed many great

conquerors to arise: the Assyrians and others, and
Israel was discomfited and defeated. And at the
very time, of course, that Mary was uttering these
words, the Jews and their land had been conquered
and possessed by the great Roman Empire. So
there they were again, as vassals once more, in
the captivity, as it were, of Rome, helpless and
hopeless. What could they do? God had allowed all
this; that was a part of his method. It comes out
so clearly, does it not? He allows apparent defeats.

Encouragements
But there is a third principle and thank God for
this. *He gives, in spite of all this, periodic encour-*
agements. The initial promise to Abraham, then
apparent forgetfulness; then forgetfulness apparently to the point where he has forsaken his people and is no longer interested or else has not the
power to help them or to deliver them. Ah yes, but
to save us from a final despair and utter hopelessness he gives periodic encouragements – 'He hath
holpen his servant Israel'; 'to his seed for ever'; 'As
he spake to our fathers'.

If you go through the Old Testament, you will
find that God in different ways repeated the
promise made to Abraham. He repeated it to
Isaac. He repeated it to Jacob. He repeated it to
Judah. He repeated it to David. It is in some of
the Psalms and in some of the prophets. Just at
any given moment God may send the message.
The people are almost giving up, and then God

sends the word reminding them of the promise. He says: 'I am still the God of Abraham; the God of Isaac and the God of Jacob.' The covenant God, the covenant-keeping God; the promise is still in force; it still avails.

And if I did not believe this, I would confess from this pulpit to being altogether without hope. If I, like some people, believed that the success and the future of the Christian Church was dependent upon human ability and power and organisation, if I believed that organised campaigns and so on were really going to solve the problem, I should be entirely hopeless.

Things are very bad, you say. What is the use of going on praying for revival? The answer is the whole of the Old Testament. This is the God in whom I believe; the God who makes a promise and then seems to forget it; allows his people to be thrown down, to be defeated, almost destroyed. There they are languishing, in hopelessness; but ,thank God, he gives us bits of encouragement. He reminds us that he is still there. We are praying for showers; thank God for an occasional droplet! Thank God for an occasional warming of the heart. Oh, it is nothing, I know. Yes, but do not despise the day of small things. The God who does the small thing is just giving you a sample of the big thing he can do. 'As he spake to our fathers' – and he still does. We are passing through a period of difficulty; we are in a wilderness; we are in a drought, but thank God for every little encouragement he gives. He reminds us that he is the God of our fathers still; the promise is sure. That is his method.

God's Time

And then my last comment under this heading is that *he obviously has his own chosen time.* Who would have anticipated that he would have sent his Son into the world at the particular moment he did? But it was then that God did it. Why? Because it was 'the fulness of the time' (see Gal. 4:4). Do not try to understand God's ways. Get hold of these principles. But if you think that you will be able to work out a plan and a scheme and say that in such and such a month, such and such a thing is to happen, you will be wrong every time. You cannot do it! God has his own time; he has his own method; he has his own appointed due moment; and when it comes he does what he said he would do.

He did not give a time to Abraham. All he told him was that he would send this Messiah out of his loins: and he did it! And he did it in his own moment. And that is to me the marvellous thing about revivals.[1] You can never prophesy revival. You can never predict it. There is always an element of surprise. Just when you think all is hopeless and you are giving up, God comes. And he does not come when you think he is going to.

---

1   This sermon was preached in 1959, which was the centenary of the great 1859 revival.

I have said it before from this pulpit: I say it again. That is what makes preaching such a romantic thing: this pulpit is the most romantic place in the world that I know of. I never know what is going to happen when I enter it. I sometimes think that something wonderful is going to happen and it does not. But I sometimes come with comparative dryness and God gives me this blessing, this shower in my soul. He has his own time. So let us learn the principles. Let us go on, let us be content knowing that God has his plan, his covenant, his purpose, and he will surely bring it to pass.

GOD'S GUARANTEE

Finally, the coming of Christ *is the guarantee of the fulfilment of all God's promises to all the seed.* We are now looking to the future. This event guarantees not only all that we have been looking at, but the whole of the future, for God's promises are not exhausted yet. There is much more to come. What Mary saw was that the birth of this Son of hers was an absolute proof of God's faithfulness to his promises, that not one of them can ever fall or fail.

Here, then, is the way to look at the future. What God did when he sent his Son into the world is an absolute guarantee that he will do everything that he has ever promised to do. Look at it in a personal sense: 'all things work together for good to them that love God' – that is a promise – 'to them who are the called according to *his* purpose' (Rom. 8:28). 'But how can I know that that is true for me?' asks someone. The answer is the Incarnation. God has given the final proof there that all his promises are sure, that he is faithful to everything he has ever said, so that promise is sure for you. Whatever your state or condition may be, whatever may come to meet you, he has said, 'I will never leave thee, nor forsake thee' (Heb. 13:5) – and he will not. He has said so, and we have an absolute proof that he fulfils his promises. He does not always do it immediately in the way that we think. No, no! But he does it! And he will never fail to do it.

SANCTIFICATION

Obviously, we have a theme here that would keep us for the rest of the day and the rest of the week. Work it out for yourselves. *Look at it in terms of your sanctification.* Are you struggling against sin; are you sometimes feeling hopeless? Here is the answer to you. '[H]e which hath begun a good work in you will perform *it* until the day of Jesus Christ' (Phil. 1:6). He is bringing many sons to glory, and if you are a child of God, if he has set his heart upon you, if you are in his plan, if you are one of his chosen, he will deal with you until you shall be finally faultless and blameless without 'spot, or wrinkle, or any such thing' (Eph. 5:27).

He will perfect you. If you are fool enough to defy him, he will chastise you. He will whip you with scorpions. He will chisel you until he gets you where he purposes to bring you. Do not fight against him therefore. '[W]hom the Lord loveth he chasteneth' (Heb. 12:6). And he is doing it for our holiness, for our sanctification. His promise is sure; it will never fail; there is no such thing as falling away from grace. If a man or woman has been given new life, it will go on to final perfection. He has sanctified forever those who come to God by him, those whom he has chosen. 'For by one offering he hath perfected for ever them that are sanctified' (Heb. 10:14).

Of course! This is God and he does not change. His purpose cannot be frustrated. Your sanctification and ultimately your glorification, is guaranteed by the Incarnation. It is difficult to realise this, is it not? But the promise to Abraham and his seed is not merely that our sins are to be forgiven and that we are to be reconciled to God. It is also that we are to be saved: entirely, completely, body, soul and spirit; perfect, without any blemish of any kind.

And, of course, it is so difficult for us to realise this. Your body is weak and frail: so is mine. There are aches and pains; the old tent is beginning to dissolve but if you are a child of God, your body will be glorified. '[W]e look for the Saviour, the Lord Jesus Christ: Who shall change our vile body, that it may be fashioned like unto his glorious body, according to the working whereby he is able even to subdue all things unto himself' (Phil. 3:20-21). What a glorious promise! 'It is all there, underwritten', says Mary, 'in this event, in this Incarnation. He has remembered his promises. He will fulfil them all because he is who and what he is.'

Gathering

Look at it then in general. Because you and I are just in a state of transition now, so is the whole Church. What is this age in which we are living? *It is the age of the gathering out of God's people from all nations under the sun.* Sometimes they come one by one; sometimes in crowds; in revivals they may come by the thousands. Yes, it has been going on for these two thousand years. God gathering out the Church. God perfecting the Church. And he will go on with it until all the fulness of the Jews and the Gentiles shall have come in and the Church will be perfect. What then? Well, then, the promise is that Christ will come again to receive these his people and to destroy all his foes.

Are you worried about the Church? Are you worried about all these rationalists and clever people? Are you beginning to fear that they will undermine the Christian faith and that everything will be lost? My dear friends, if you do, you have not understood the meaning of the Incarnation.

Think of the two thousand years that elapsed since the promise to Abraham; look at the defeats to which the children of Israel were subjected; look at the utter hopelessness. It is still the same God.

Place

The Church is in eclipse at the moment, but what does it matter? It is God's! *And the Church will be brought to the place which God has purposed for her.* Christ will come again. And he will come, probably as he did the first time, when we will all feel utterly hopeless and filled with despair and say that the Church is finished and that nothing can be done. He will come and he will scatter his enemies. He will put down the proud and the mighty, he will hurl them down from their seats; he will fill the hungry with good things and the rich he will send empty away. He will come to judge the world in righteousness; and evil and sin and hell and Satan and everything shall be cast into the lake of fire and of burning for all eternity. And he will usher in his glorious kingdom, his eternal kingdom of glory and of might and of power. He will be over all and he will then finally hand the kingdom back to the Father.

And you and I, Christian people, will be in that kingdom and in that glory. We shall judge the world. We shall judge angels. We shall share in the glory and the triumph of the Son of God. God has promised this. It is a part of the promise to Abraham. And God's method is patently still the same as it was through the days of the Old Testament dispensation. He appears to forget, and the world ridicules. They say, 'Where is the promise of his coming?' (2 Pet. 3:4). And the answer which we still give is this: that God is God, that he is not like man; that with him a thousand years are as one day, and one day as a thousand years. He has his time. He has his method. In his wisdom he allows many things to happen to his people for their own perfection, for teaching them, for their discipline and for his own final glory.

And as he sent his Son out of the womb of Mary when the fulness of the times had come, he will send him again out of heaven, riding the clouds accompanied by the holy angels.

> Jesus shall reign where'er the sun
> Doth his successive journeys run;
> His kingdom stretch from shore to shore,
> Till moons shall wax and wane no more.
>
> Isaac Watts

'In remembrance of his mercy to Abraham and to his seed for ever. As he spake to our fathers.' Thank God, the Incarnation is the final proof of the faithfulness of God, the guarantee that his every promise will be completely fulfilled.

4

THE CHRISTIAN'S EXPERIENCE

'And Mary said, My soul doth magnify the Lord, And my spirit hath rejoiced in God my Saviour. For he hath regarded the low estate of his handmaiden: for, behold, from henceforth all generations shall call me blessed. For he that is mighty hath done to me great things; and holy *is* his name' (Luke 1:46-49).

I do not really want to confine my attention to those verses. I rather want to look at the whole statement from a particular angle and standpoint. I am anxious to look at it as an expression of the consciousness of Mary of what was happening to her, of what God has done, and was doing, and was going to do to her and for her and in and through her.

Now my reason for doing this is that this is the last Sunday night of an old year. You may say: 'What's that got to do with the spiritual realm?' In a sense, of course, it has nothing to do with it, and yet we are still in the flesh, we are still in time. And so we think in terms of time, and it is not a bad thing for us, now and again, to do with respect to the spiritual realm what we do in a more ordinary realm. I refer, of course, to the habit of taking stock: to the habit of examining the position, the situation, in order that we may discover exactly where we stand. Nothing is easier in life in this world than just to go on from day to day and week to week and month to month and year to year, without stopping to consider what it all means, what it really is all about and what it will all lead to. It is so easy to be governed by circumstances and surroundings and events and happenings. We are always proposing to look into these things but somehow we do not find the time, something else comes in, and so it often goes by default.

And this can happen also in the spiritual realm. It is possible, alas, for us even to attend a place of worship Sunday by Sunday and yet not really to face the real purpose and object and function in so doing. There are still people in the world – although it is no longer in general the habit and custom for people to attend a place of worship –

who do that out of mere habit and custom, or for various other personal reasons. There are many motives that bring people to the house of God. We all know that perfectly well when we are honest with ourselves.

LISTENING TO THE GOSPEL

But the question is, have we come face to face with the real object, the real purpose? What has listening to the gospel meant to us? Not a bad question to ask, is it, at the end of an old year? How many times have you heard the gospel during the past year? Well, what has it done to you? Has it done anything? Has it made any vital difference to you? It is meant to! It is meant to change everything. '[I]f any man *be* in Christ,' says the apostle Paul, '*he is* a new creature: old things are passed away; behold, all things are become new' (2 Cor. 5:17). That is Christianity. Our Lord talks about it as a rebirth, being 'born again'. That is the effect of this gospel when it comes truly.

Has it come to us like that? Has it made any difference to us? Is it not a terrible thing that it is possible for us thus to go on listening to the gospel, and yet, in a sense, to be so detached and remote that it does nothing to us and we might just as well never have heard it. That is a terrible state to be in. And that is not my own personal opinion; our Lord himself put this very plainly on one occasion. He said that in the end we shall be judged by our response and reaction to this word, to this gospel. They are very solemn words. He said that all men and women would eventually have to face this word of his and they would have to give an answer! '[I]f any man hear my words, and believe not, I judge him not: for I came not to judge the world, but to save the world. He that rejecteth me, and receiveth not my words, hath one that judgeth him: the word that I have spoken, the same shall judge him in the last day' (John 12:47, 48).

That is a very solemnising thought. There is nothing more serious than to listen to this gospel, the preaching of this gospel, because, according to our Lord, it will meet us again. We will have to give an answer, if we have ever heard it, and the question will be why did we not believe it? We shall be confronted by Christian people, by those who did believe it, and we will be left without an excuse. They sat in the same chapel, in the same church: they heard the same gospel, the same message, the same everything. They were saved by it, why were not we? That is what he is saying. So, surely it is of vital importance to us that we should know exactly where we stand with regard to this gospel.

EXPERIENCING GRACE

Let us look at it like this: to be a Christian means that we have had an experience of the grace of God. That is essential Christianity. There are many other definitions that one could give of it.

One which I have often quoted because it seems to me to be such an excellent one is that old definition of Henry Scougal, the Scotsman who lived nearly three hundred years ago. He said that Christianity is 'the life of God in the soul of men'. In other words, what makes us Christian is not primarily what we do, but what God does to us. That is essential Christianity. This rebirth, this being born again is all God's action; that is not man's, it is God's. It is being born from above. It is the work of the Holy Spirit of God. Therefore, the essential thing about being a Christian is that one has thus been dealt with by God, and that is an experience. It is not only experience, of course; there is the element of understanding, and so many other things. But the vital thing is just this experience.

Now I am contrasting this, obviously, with many other things which so often pass as Christianity. I have mentioned them many and many a time before, I know, but I am taking no risks. We are examining ourselves in the light of our Lord's warning, and one can never repeat it too frequently.

First, then, being interested in Christianity does not alone make us Christians. You can take an intellectual interest in these things. There is nothing more fascinating than that. This is the most amazing system of truth in the world or that the world has ever known. It is a fascinating, intellectual occupation to study the Bible and books about it. Many people have gone through life doing that without being Christians. You can be interested intellectually and intellectually only.

Then there are the people who think that being Christian means doing good. That is popular today. People who do good, they say, are Christians though they themselves may say that they are Muslims or Hindus, and that does not matter! Though they may not say that they are Christians, they are, they must be. That is what makes us Christian – what we do, doing good. But that, of course, is the exact opposite of all we find in the Bible.

Other people believe it is attending church services, particularly if you get up early in the morning to do so, and adopt certain postures and things like that. 'Oh, that's fine: that's wonderful! Christianity! Exceptional!' But it is still something you do, whereas the basic definition is that it is that which God does to us. It is an experience.

So let us examine ourselves in the light of that, using what we are told here by Mary with regard to her experience. Let us use her statement as a means of self-examination that we may test ourselves. For I suggest to you that it can be said that in many ways Mary's experience, as reported here, is the first authentic Christian experience. She tells us about her reaction to what God had done to her. You say, 'That is different because she was going to give birth to a child', but that is not the important thing in Mary's experience, as she explains herself. She does not refer much to that. No, no, the important thing is Mary's realisation of what is happening, of what God is doing. That is the thing to which she gives expression in the Magnificat. In other words, Mary is aware of undergoing a spiritual experience, and she gives us here in her statement the salient, cardinal features and elements in this Christian experience.

No Standard Experience

So let us look at it together in this way. Let us first of all get rid of something which is so often a stumbling block to people, and that is the element of time in this experience, or, to put it still more generally, the way in which this experience comes. I have known many people who have doubted whether they were Christians or not because the experience had not come to them in a given way or manner. This is a very subtle snare by which the devil robs many people of their joy. He would have us believe that there is a standard experience, and one only, and that unless we have had that exact experience, we are not Christians at all. But I feel that this one story alone is enough to tell us that there is no such thing as a standardised Christian experience. Sometimes that experience may come very suddenly, but sometimes it may come very gradually; and the thing that I am anxious to emphasise is that it does not matter to the slightest extent whether it is sudden or gradual. What matters is that it has happened.

But this, I repeat, does worry certain people. Imagine somebody, for instance, reading John Bunyan's *Grace Abounding*. There you read that poor John Bunyan, for eighteen months, passed through a terrible agony of repentance. He was conscious of his sin, his unworthiness and his shame. It was such an agony in his soul that he tells us quite solemnly that on one occasion he felt he could even smell brimstone in the air; he felt such a wretch. He was so unhappy on another occasion that when he happened to see a number of geese grazing in a field nearby, he envied them. He wished he were an animal. He wished he was not capable of this awful agony through which he was passing, his agony of repentance which went on for all those months. And there are some people who think that if you do not go through that precise experience, you have never been a Christian. They even emphasise the eighteen months almost, and unless you conform to the pattern, they say, you are not a Christian. Now there is no scriptural basis for that whatsoever.

Others read an account of the Philippian jailor, or something like that, and find a man suddenly converted, and unless it happens to them like that, if they have to go through remorse and repentance for eighteen months instead of seeing it suddenly, they feel they are not Christians; they say that it must be sudden. So some say gradual and some say sudden, but, again, the answer is that there is no standardised experience taught in the New Testament. The case of Mary that we are looking at, as we have seen, is most instructive in this respect; thank God for it. So I am holding it before you in order that I may perchance comfort somebody who is in trouble about this matter.

Mary's Reaction

Did you notice what happened to Mary? The archangel came and made the announcement, and instead of jumping at it and taking to it with both hands, Mary stumbled at it and queried and questioned it.

Questioning

Instead of her being filled with a spirit of rejoicing at first, I read this: 'when she saw *him*, she was troubled at his saying, and cast in her mind what manner of salutation this should be' (Luke 1:29). She was stumbling. The archangel went on speaking, but even then Mary did not grasp it. He told her about this wonderful child that was to be born of her, and again, instead of praising God, Mary said to the angel: 'How shall this be, seeing I know not a man?' She said, in effect: 'You are talking nonsense, it is impossible; how can I bear a child, I am a virgin, I have never known a man, I am not married?' She stumbled. That was Mary's *first* reaction: *questioning and doubting*.

Resignation

And then she went on to the *second* step. When the archangel had answered her doubts and mildly rebuked her, and told her that with God nothing shall be impossible, Mary said: 'Behold, the handmaid of the Lord; be it unto me according to thy word. And the angel departed from her.' She did not get further. That is a sort of *passive resignation*. She had not seen it yet, but she had seen that she had been rebuked for querying the possibility of this thing wtih God; she had been rebuked for putting a limit to the almightiness of God; and she said, 'I see I am wrong; I don't understand, but I will submit'. She went through that stage, and it was only later when she heard the words of Elisabeth, her cousin, the mother of John the Baptist, that she saw it. And the moment she did so, she burst forth into this Magnificat.

So you see the steps and stages, hindrances and obstacles, which she had to overcome. It was a kind of process through which she passed. She did not say, immediately she heard the message of the archangel, 'I believe; it is wonderful'.

I repeat, then, that the thing that matters is not whether this has happened to you suddenly or gradually; the vital thing is, has it happened? In order that I may help you, let me use an illustration which I once heard an old, old preacher using and which I thought was very good. He said, 'Think of two men going on a journey walking along a road. One of them is walking in a sort of gentle drizzle, but he has a long journey to take and as a result of this gentle drizzle, which has gone on throughout the whole journey, he arrives at his destination wet through.

'The other man sets out in the glorious sunshine, and for the first three hours of his walk he is continuing in this sunshine. Suddenly, the clouds gather when he has only about half a mile to go and a cloudburst takes place, and in a few moments he is soaked through to the skin.

'They both arrive at their destination wet, soaked through. It took a long time in one case; it happened very quickly and suddenly in the second. But, you see, what matters is not whether you got wet suddenly or gradually, but the fact that you got wet through to the skin.' So God forbid that anybody should be stumbled by that particular point. It does not matter how nor when, the mode nor the method: the vital question is, has it happened?

ELEMENTS

Secondly then, what are the elements in this experience as taught in this incident? They are all here.

Awareness

The *first* is *an awareness of being dealt with and being blessed by God*. Mary puts that right at the beginning: 'For he hath regarded the low estate of his handmaiden ... For he that is mighty hath done to me great things; and holy *is* his name' (vv. 48-49). 'Ah, but', you say again, 'there, of course, she is referring to the fact that she is going to have this child.' I know it comes in, but that is not what Mary is most aware of. What she is

95

aware of above everything else is that God has been doing something to her. That is the thing to emphasise. If to be a Christian means to receive life from God; if to be a Christian means that you are born again; if to be a Christian means that you have passed into life, from darkness to light, that you are a new creature, a new creation, then is it not quite inevitable that anyone to whom that has happened must be aware of the fact that something is happening?

It is not a decision that I take, it is not something that I do; it is not the end product of my activity. No, no! The particular thing about this is that as Mary was aware that God was doing something to her, so the person who has become a Christian has the same awareness. Though you do not understand it, you are aware that something is happening to you; something is taking place in your life; you are being disturbed. I have borrowed those words of Wordsworth before now; he did not mean what I mean but I can use them, in a sense. He put it like this: I have felt a presence that disturbs me with the joy of elevated thoughts. That is it – *'felt a presence'*.

You cannot be a Christian without being aware that God is dealing with you, is concerned about you, is doing something to you. God has his hands upon you. You may at first react in a hostile manner against that; you may not like it; you may want to shake it off. That has often happened. Many people have done that. But whether you like it or not, you are aware that something is happening. You may wish sometimes that you had never heard of God, that you had never heard of Christ; you wish you could be enjoying that other life with the world as you have always done; but something has come in, you are disturbed. Sometimes it is nothing more than that at the beginning – just an uneasiness, just an awareness that something is troubling you and has come into you. You wish you could divest yourself of it, but you cannot, it is something inside you. It is the one who made you at the beginning making you again; his hands and fingers are upon you and moulding you.

Mary, then, was aware of being dealt with by God and so is every Christian. You may fight and kick and struggle, and yet the whole time you know that it is not you, it is something else. That is why, in a sense, I always feel happier about a man who is militantly opposed to Christianity and is fighting with his teeth clenched and hating it. I almost prefer him to the man who feels that he, by living a good life and this and that, is making himself a Christian. With regard to that second man, I am not aware that God is doing anything to him at all; *he* is doing everything. He is like the Pharisee who thanks God for all he is doing. But when this other man is struggling against it, and I see him kicking violently, I say to myself very often: 'I see God is doing something to that man.'

But let me give a word of comfort to someone who may be very anxious about someone who is dear to them. You may be thinking that that one is going further and further away, you say he has become more and more violent in his opposition. It may be the best sign in the world! What is he doing? Ah, he is trying to get rid of this power that has started dealing with him. It is God acting. He does not understand: he does not like it; he is against it so far. But there it is; God has put his hand upon him. Hold on! That is the first thing.

Surprise

The *second* is – and it follows quite inevitably from the first – the element of *surprise and amazement*. It is here everywhere in Mary's statement: 'My soul doth magnify the Lord, And my spirit hath rejoiced in God my Saviour. For he hath regarded the low estate of his handmaiden: for, behold, from henceforth all generations shall call me blessed. For he that is mighty hath done to me great things; and holy *is* his name.' Do you not feel and hear the note of amazement and of astonishment?

Again I would emphasise and underline this. Mary could not believe this thing that was happening to her. It was so remarkable. It was so astonishing. She knew it was happening, but she could scarcely credit it. 'Should this happen to me? My low estate? A handmaiden? Is it happening?' Yes, it is! But she can scarcely contain herself. The surprise and the amazement at it all, that

God had ever looked upon her and had chosen to do this to her.

I almost feel that this is the acid test. Are you surprised, amazed at yourself? You never will be, of course, until you are conscious that God is doing something to you. Ah, you can be very moral: there is no amazement in that. You decided to do it and you are doing it – intellectual interest and all the rest of it. There is nothing to amaze us in that. We are doing it volitionally, willingly and well aware of what we are doing. There is no element of surprise and amazement until we are conscious that God is doing something to us, and then we are filled with amazement, as Mary was, and we, too, ask, 'Can this be true of me? Is it really I? Is this happening to me?'

I mean something like this: the moment this process begins to go on in you, you will find tremendous changes taking place. You will find, for instance, that whereas you never gave a single thought to the fact that you have a soul, it is now your chief concern. You never gave a thought to the fact of death; you often think about it now. You never gave a thought to the next world and the life beyond; you regarded that as morbid, something to be dismissed, never to be thought of, but now it is very frequently in your mind.

The Bible was to you the most boring book in the world. The idea of reading the Bible for pleasure was quite unthinkable, of course! But now you find yourself wanting to read it and you desire to understand it. It is the book of books to you, and so on. Prayer! You never prayed at all unless, of course, you were desperately ill or somebody dear to you was desperately ill; or some terrible accident or calamity took place; or there was a war: then, of course, you prayed. But when things were going well, you would not dream of praying. However, now you see that prayer is the most amazing and wonderful thing in the world, and what you cannot get over is that you should be trying to pray. 'Is it possible? Am I the same person? Can it be I? The thing seems ... But no, no,' you say, 'why not?' And Mary felt all that: this amazement, this astonishment, this surprising element.

And you find this, of course, in every one of these New Testament writers. Take the classic example of it, the apostle Paul himself: 'I live: yet not I' (Gal. 2:20). 'There is something wrong here,' says Paul. 'I live – yet not I; I am Saul of Tarsus: I am not Saul of Tarsus. Saul of Tarsus was a blasphemer, an injurious person, a hater of Christ and of the gospel. I cannot be Saul of Tarsus, and yet I am Saul of Tarsus. I know I am. I am the same man.' You see, he is in trouble; he does not understand himself. 'I live, yet not I.'

Now that is Christianity. Here is a man who is amazed at himself. He cannot understand himself. There is only one solution: 'I live; yet not I, but Christ liveth in me'. And he could not get over the fact that the Son of God, the Lord Jesus

Christ, whom he had blasphemed and hated and whom he had reviled should have loved him with an everlasting love and should have died for him. '[T]he Son of God,' he says, 'who loved me, and gave himself for me.' He never got over it. Never!

And that is essential Christian experience. Yes, says Charles Wesley, you are perfectly right:

> And can it be that I should gain
> An interest in the Saviour's blood?
> Died He for me, who caused His pain?
> For me, who Him to death pursued?
> Amazing love! how can it be
> That Thou, my God, shouldst die for me?

Has this happened to me? That is what Mary was saying: the amazement, the surprise. Are you surprised at yourself? Are you driven to say, like the apostle Paul elsewhere, 'But by the grace of God I am what I am' (1 Cor. 15:10)? I cannot explain it; that is the only explanation. I do not understand myself, I have undergone such a complete revolution. I was against, I am now for. With a vehemence with which I once persecuted, I am now preaching. A complete transformation, a new creature, new creation. And no Christian can ever get over the surprise.

Here we are, a little company on this last Sunday night of this old year; let me tell you that nothing so amazes me as that I am in this pulpit and doing what I am doing at this moment. Why am I here? Was it because I was a good man?

Certainly not! Was it because I decided? Certainly not! I am what I am by the grace of God, and I am more and more amazed at the fact that I should be preaching like this. I might so easily have been doing something else. I never decided. I fought against. This is God's action.

Why should any Christian be different from anybody else? Why should we not all be living the way of the world? Living to drink and to dance and to indulge our baser passions? Why not? It is not because we are any better. It is not because we have a superior understanding. It is not because of anything in us. We are what we are by the grace of God, and what is amazing is that we are his in spite of ourselves. It is God's action. It is what he is doing. That is what Mary felt.

Humility
Then, *thirdly*, because of this – and you see how each point leads to the next – you notice her *humility* and her *lowliness*. '[H]e hath regarded the low estate of his handmaiden ... he that is mighty hath done to me great things; and holy *is* his name' (vv. 48, 49). Of course! Where there is a complete absence of humility and lowliness, there is no Christianity at all.

I have reminded you that Mary here antici-pates the Beatitudes, and they are, you remember: 'Blessed *are* the poor in spirit ... Blessed *are* they that mourn ... Blessed *are* the meek ... Blessed *are* they which do hunger and thirst after righteous-

ness' (Matt. 5:3-6). They are the Christians. That
is Christianity.

Is it not inevitable that a Christian should feel
like this? These things need no demonstration;
they need no argument. What Mary was
conscious of was this: 'My soul doth magnify
the Lord, And my spirit hath rejoiced in God my
Saviour.' She had felt the touch of his power.
The archangel had told her that she would: that
the All-Highest would over-cover her and that
the power of God should be upon her, and she
had felt it. She had, as it were, touched God. She
had sensed the eternal presence and I do not
care who you are or what you are, if you have
ever had the faintest suspicion of a realisation
of the presence and the glory and the greatness
and the majesty and the holiness of God, it will
humble you to the dust.

You will feel that you are vile and unworthy
– humility, lowliness. Mary was not proud of
herself in any way at all. Christians never are: not
proud of their works; not proud of their activity;
not proud of their morality; not proud of their
prayers; not proud of their understanding. What
Christians are conscious of above everything else
is their own complete, utter unworthiness. That
this should happen to me! Elisabeth felt the same
thing. She was filled with the Holy Spirit and she
spoke out with a loud voice and said, 'Blessed *art*
thou among women, and blessed is the fruit of thy
womb. And whence *is* this to me, that the mother

of my Lord should come to me?' That is it! And Mary feels exactly the same thing.

The moment we realise something of the nearness and the presence and the character of God's being, we see ourselves as we are, in all our nakedness, all our sinfulness, all our unrighteousness and all our unworthiness. Isaiah, for example, was a very good man, but he was given that vision, that glimpse of God, and he said at once, 'Woe *is* me! for I am undone; because I *am* a man of unclean lips, and I dwell in the midst of a people of unclean lips' (Isa. 6:5).

Again, the bold, self-confident and self-satisfied Simon Peter, the disciple, said the same thing – Peter the daredevil, Peter the man who was ready to venture in and be the first volunteer always. Yes, but on one occasion he had been out fishing with the others and they had caught nothing. Then our Lord just gave them a command and they carried it out and they caught so many fish that they did not know what to do with them. Do you remember the effect on Simon Peter? He went to our Lord and he said, 'Depart from me; for I am a sinful man, O Lord' (Luke 5:8). What made him feel he was so sinful and vile? Oh, he had had a glimpse of the almightiness of the Lord Jesus Christ, the Son of God, the manifestation of divine power, and it made him feel he was vile and unworthy.

I do not see how men and women have a right to regard themselves as Christians unless they see something of their own unworthiness and sinfulness, their own weakness, their own lack of power. The people about whom I am absolutely certain that they are not Christians are those who think they can make themselves Christians. But you give me men and women who are conscious of their unworthiness; you give me people who say, 'Oh, if you but knew my heart, if you knew my thoughts and imaginations; if you knew me as I am within, you would not regard me as a Christian', then I am very hopeful about them.

If you feel that you deserve to be forgiven, I do not think you are forgiven. If you feel you deserve to be blessed by God, I am sure you are not being blessed by God. No, these are the people – 'That this should happen to me!' Humility. Unworthiness. A sense, therefore, of it all coming from God in spite of our wretchedness and our vileness. You again say with Charles Wesley:

Just and holy is Thy Name,
I am all unrighteousness,
Vile and full of sin I am,
Thou art full of truth and grace.

Gratitude
Then the *fourth* point, of course, is gratitude and praise. 'My soul doth magnify the Lord'. Of course!

Praise my soul, the King of Heaven,
To His feet thy tribute bring.

Why?

Ransomed, healed, restored, forgiven,
Who like thee His praise should sing?
Praise Him! Praise Him!
Praise the everlasting King.

Henry Francis Lyte

My dear friends, have you a sense of gratitude to God? Is there a glimmering of praise in your heart somewhere? Is there something within you that makes you desire to praise God and to magnify his grace? Is it possible to be a Christian without feeling something of that? Do you believe your sins are forgiven? Do you believe your soul is redeemed? Do you say that you have got a new nature? Do you say that there is a blessed hope set, awaiting you in heaven with God? Do you believe all that?

Do you really believe that Jesus of Nazareth, the babe of Bethlehem, first of all was, in reality, the Son of God? Do you really believe in the Incarnation? Do you really believe that 'God so loved the world, that he gave his only begotten Son'; sent him into the world, sent him into the virgin's womb, sent him to be born as a babe in that stable and put into the manger? Do you believe that God so loved you that he sent his Son not only to do that but to die on the cross on Calvary's hill and to take your sins upon him, and to receive their punishment that you might be absolved and forgiven and reconciled to God, and made his child, and given an everlasting life?

Do you really believe it? How can you believe it without feeling some sense of gratitude and of praise and of thanksgiving?

Do you feel a little of it? I want to try and help you. Is there the faintest flicker of a sense of gratitude within you? If so, you can be hopeful. But if you can consider these blessed facts; if you can consider the Christmas event, the Incarnation and all that followed; if you can look at it with a complete detachment, with a philosophical or intellectual objectivity; and if it does not move you even to the slightest fraction; if there is not a speck of softness in your calloused, hard heart, how can you be a Christian? O no! The one who realises what God is doing and what is happening says, 'My soul doth magnify the Lord, And my spirit hath rejoiced in God my Saviour.'

Fear

The next step is *fear*. 'Yes,' says Mary, 'his mercy is on them that fear him from generation to generation.' What is this? It is not a craven fear. It is not the fear of hell. It is not the fear of punishment here. It is what the author of the Epistle to the Hebrews calls 'reverence and godly fear' (Heb. 12:28). It is, in other words, that sense of God about which I have been speaking. This, again, is a very good test. People of the world, those who are obviously not Christians, know nothing about the fear of the Lord; but I will give you a good and a comforting negative test in order to help you. If you have a consciousness within you that the eye of God is upon you, wherever you are and whatever you are doing, it is hopeful.

Christians are men and women who walk in the fear of the Lord. They say: 'It is not other people that matter; it is not I myself that matter. I know that God's eye is upon me and that I am ever under God. God is ever looking at me and I cannot escape him. I know that "his mercy *is* on them that fear him from generation to generation" (Luke 1:50).' This is a healthy and a hopeful fear. It is what the apostle Paul means when he says, '[W]ork out your own salvation with fear and trembling.' He says that to Christian people. '[W]ork out your own salvation with fear and trembling. For it is God which worketh in you both to will and to do of *his* good pleasure' (Phil. 2:12, 13). The only man or woman who can know fear and trembling in this sense is a Christian. The others know nothing about it. Take your typical 'man of the world': the man who is lauded on the radio and the television, the freeloader, the drinker, the gambler, the man who indulges in sex. Fear and trembling – they know nothing about it! They will know though; they will know, and they will know to all eternity if they die like that. But now they know nothing about it.

But Christians do know something about it. It is the fear that people are aware of when they are afraid of hurting someone whom they love. That is the fear. Not the fear of a law, but the fear of

love; the fear of hurting or wounding love; the fear
of disappointing love; the fear and trembling. It is
because they have some realisation of God's being,
his holiness, his majesty, his glory, his greatness
and his eternity. And Christians realise that they
are ever in the presence of God. They walk care-
fully. They walk softly. They walk in the fear of
the Lord.

Joy

And, *lastly*, the Christian is one who *rejoices* in
the Lord Jesus Christ. Yes, Mary had come to see
that this child that was to be born of her was the
Son of God. She said: 'All generations shall call me
blessed.' 'I, of everybody, have been chosen to have
this inestimable privilege of being the mother of
the Son of God. As the archangel told me, the one
who is to be born of my womb is the Son of God.'
And in anticipation she gloried in him and rejoiced
in him.

That is the final test of whether we are Christians
or not, that our entire hope is centred on the Son
of God, the Lord Jesus Christ. The Mohammedan
and the Jew believe in God. But what makes men
and women Christians is not to believe in God
only, but to believe in God through Christ. To
realise that it is Christ alone who can bring them
to God. It is Christ alone who reconciles them to
God. It is Christ alone who gives them this new
nature and makes them 'partakers of the divine
nature' (2 Pet. 1:4). They rejoice in God.

The apostle Peter wrote, 'Whom having not seen, ye love; in whom, though now ye see *him* not, yet believing, ye rejoice with joy unspeakable and full of glory' (1 Pet. 1:8). Can you say,

I rest my faith in Him alone
Who died for my transgressions to atone.

Can you say with the apostle Paul: 'God forbid that I should glory, save in the cross of our Lord Jesus Christ, by whom the world is crucified unto me, and I unto the world' (Gal. 6:14)? Can you say 'In the cross of Christ I glory'; do you make that your boast? Do you rejoice entirely and only in him? Those are the elements of this Christian experience. Mary was aware of them, and everybody who becomes a Christian must be aware of them in exactly the same way.

Encouragement
So, I end with this final word of encouragement to you. If you are in trouble at this point, if my sermon has made you unhappy; if you feel that these tests are difficult to answer, let me say this to you: are you in trouble, I wonder, because you are still in Mary's first stage?

Trouble
Are you in that condition in which you have not yet realised that here you are in a realm that is altogether different from everything that is known by the world. You are in a spiritual realm here.

Mary stumbled because she did not realise that she was being addressed by an archangel and that he was talking about a miracle, about the action of God, the supernatural, the spiritual realm. She had not realised that, so she stumbled and she was trying to understand it all.

So I wonder whether that is your trouble. Do not bring the canons that you employ in business or in your profession here: they will not help you; they will be of no value. When Christ came into this world, as the apostle Paul reminds us, 'the princes of this world' did not know him. They were the great men, the philosophers and others, but they did not know him, 'for had they known *it*, they would not have crucified the Lord of glory' (1 Cor. 2:8). Why not? Because they were trying to understand him and they could not. This is God's activity; it is God sending his Son, doing the work by the Spirit. Dismiss all your categories of thought. Realise that you are in a new and in a different and in a spiritual realm.

GIVING UP TRYING TO UNDERSTAND

Then, secondly, give up trying to understand it. You never will! '[G]reat is the mystery of godliness' (1 Tim. 3:16). Christ is the eternal mystery. Two natures in one person. You cannot understand it! Do not try to! Do not be a fool. New birth? Of course you cannot understand it. It is God's miracle, like the wind – do not try to. What then are you to do? Well, emulate Mary's example. O, you may feel baffled but if, at any rate, you have now come to see that is what God does and not what you do, then, follow Mary and say, all right, carry on. That is what she said in effect. 'Behold the handmaid of the Lord; be it unto me according to thy word.' Just as you are, not understanding, baffled, bewildered, perplexed. If you are conscious that God has started something in your life, stop trying to understand, just turn to him and say: 'Go on, go on, I submit.' Allow him to go on speaking. Allow him to go on acting. Simply do what he tells you. Obey what you are beginning to feel within you. Go on. And if God has started dealing with you, he will not give it up. He will bring you to the point when some Elisabeth will say something to you, and you will know that you have been born again.

You will be amazed at yourself; astonished; surprised. You will be humbled, feel humiliated, and yet you will rejoice in it and glory in it. You will praise God, and you will give all the glory to his dearly beloved, only begotten Son, 'Who, being in the form of God, thought it not robbery to be equal with God: But made himself of no reputation' (Phil. 2:6-7). He was born as a babe in Bethlehem and put in a manger and went willingly to the death on the cross for you. You will give him all the glory, and you will say, 'Amazing though it is, I am what I am by the grace of God.'

Thanks be unto God for his unspeakable gift.